The Self after Postmodernity

THE SELF
AFTER POSTMODERNITY

CALVIN O. SCHRAG

Yale University Press   New Haven and London

Set in Caslon type by Tseng Information Systems, Inc.,
Durham, North Carolina
Printed in the United States of America.

Library of Congress Cataloging-in-Publication Data

Schrag, Calvin O.
The self after postmodernity / Calvin O. Schrag.
p.   cm.
Includes index.
ISBN 0-300-06842-5 (alk. paper)
1. Self (Philosophy)   2. Postmodernism.   I. Title.
BD438.5.S37   1997
126—dc20   96-38600
CIP

A catalogue record for this book is
available from the British Library.

The paper in this book meets the guidelines
for permanence and durability of the Committee
on Production Guidelines for Book Longevity of
the Council on Library Resources.

10 9 8 7 6 5 4 3 2 1

To my grandson
Luke Mathew Stampfl
whose journey on the road to selfhood is just beginning

CONTENTS

Preface

The text that follows was originally presented at Trent University, Peterborough, Ontario, as the 1995 Gilbert Ryle Lectures. Since the lectures were delivered, the text has undergone modifications of various sorts, designed principally to transpose the lecturer-hearer format into an author-reader format.

Endowments for lectureships by sundry individuals and agencies have become increasingly common at North American colleges and universities over the years. These lectureships have been established for the expressed purpose of bringing ideas to a wider public, including not only scholars within a variety of disciplines at a given institution but also persons outside the walls of the college or university proper. It is assumed that the lectures will both have interdisciplinary appeal and be of interest to the intelligent and informed layperson. A lectureship of this sort provides some respite from the hyper-specialization, often accompanied by isolating and discipline-specific vocabularies, that has increasingly become a trademark of modern academe. Given such conditions, the responsibility laid upon the lecturer is considerable. He or she is called upon to forge lines of communication across several academic disciplines and explore the relevance of the topic of the lectureship for citizens of a public world.

The designated topic for the Gilbert Ryle Lectures at Trent University has customarily been drawn from the field of philosophy, the intent being to pay homage to the legacy of one of the more illustrious philosophers of the twentieth century.

That philosophers would from time to time be called upon to bring philosophy to the general public surely ought not to be surprising to those who have some knowledge of the history of the discipline. We need but to recall the Athenian Socrates, who at the dawn of Western philosophy exemplified the life of philosophical inquiry in dramatic manner by mingling with the citizens of Athens in the local marketplace, engaging them in conversations about the achievement of self-knowledge and eliciting from them arguments on how best to conduct one's personal and public life. This definition of the philosophical task, along the lines of a rhetoric of inquiry directed *to* the public and crafted *for* the public, should not be taken as an invitation to popularize by leveling thought to its lowest common denominator. It does, however, provide a motivation to communicate what one considers to be of philosophical importance and interest to a general audience and a wide readership.

The Socratic challenge for addressing the public has certain implications for attaining that delicate balance of the spoken and the written word. On the current philosophical scene, as even the casual observer has been in position to notice, there is an intensified interest in contrasting voice and text, speaking and writing, hearing and reading. These are often presented as bipolar oppositions, inviting a tendency to choose the one or the other as primary and privileged. In some circles we are warned about the dangers of phonocentrism; in other circles we are told about the perils of pantextualism. If the one is the Scylla and the other the Charybdis, then we had best heed advice on how to maneuver between them. It may indeed be that the most effective way to achieve such a feat is to solicit contributions from both phonality and textuality without reducing the sense and significance of the one to the other, attending to the strategies of a rhetoric of public address without sacrificing the guidelines of a rhetoric of composition. The passage from the diction of the spoken word in lecture hall and popular assembly to the syntax of the written word in treatise and tract—and from the latter back to the former—could then be understood in terms of a dynamics of complementarity and mutual enrichment. Such a complementarity would stand to remind speakers and writers of the entwinement of what is said and what is written.

There is also a yet more specific reason for remembering that this book began as a series of lectures. This fact contributes to an explanation not only of the style but also of some of the themes and arguments that I proffer in the continuing discourse. One would think it only a fair-minded gesture for a lecturer, invited to fulfill the conditions of a lectureship honoring the life and career of a distinguished scholar, researcher, or creative artist, to link in some manner the contents of her or his public address to the accomplishments of the designated honoree. Clearly, this does not mean that the rendered lectures need follow the format of an exposition or critical analysis of the work of the celebrity in whose name the endowment has been established. Surely readers would be misled were they to expect in the text that follows a discussion of the consummate philosophical contribution of Gilbert Ryle. Yet I have made a special effort to include Ryle as a sometimes interlocutor in the story that I have to tell.

The historians of twentieth-century philosophy have already secured a niche for Gilbert Ryle as a leading representative of twentieth-century analytical philosophy. What tends to be overlooked, however, is his role in the critical reception of continental philosophy by the Anglo-American philosophical world. He was one of the first of his profession to write a review of Martin Heidegger's epoch-making *Sein und Zeit* shortly after its publication. Although critical of certain developments in Heidegger's treatise, Ryle was at the same time laudatory of the principal thrust of the project, commending Heidegger as a philosopher who "shows himself to be a thinker of real importance by the immense subtlety and searchingness of his examination of consciousness, by the boldness and originality of his methods and conclusions, and by the unflagging energy with which he tries to think beyond the stock categories of orthodox philosophy and psychology" (*Mind: A Quarterly Review of Psychology and Philosophy*, vol. 38, 1929, p. 370).

From this we learn, and pretty much straightaway, that Ryle understood precisely Heidegger's central project of deconstruction (*Abbau*), wherewith one is challenged to think beyond the classical conceptual schemes that have become normative for the Western philosophical tradition. This is precisely what is at issue in Heidegger's call for a deconstruction or dismantling of the metaphysical and epistemological constructs that have informed the history of occidental philosophy from its beginning. And was it not such a similar strategy of deconstruction or dismantling that Ryle himself put into service twenty years later in his critique of the Cartesian construct of mind as a ghost in a machine?

Gilbert Ryle's highly praised work *The Concept of Mind* may indeed find a place in the history of twentieth-century philosophy as one of the early illustrations of deconstructionist thought. To be sure, it may sound odd to the ears of contemporary philosophers to hear the name *Ryle* and the word *deconstruction* in some manner of juxtaposition. But the annals of philosophy are replete with truths that upon initial presentation have had about them a ring of oddity.

At various junctures in the following narratives I shall bring Ryle into the conversation, not simply because the ideas in this book were originally presented in the form of lectures that bear his name and require an acknowledgment of his philosophical legacy, but principally because the chosen topic has affinities with his long-standing preoccupation with the problem of selfhood. Although my intermittent conversations with him at times take a critical turn, and in the end his concept of the self is not mine, I hope that the discussions that follow might stand as a tribute to Ryle's pioneering work in shaping the problem of mind in current philosophical discourse.

Many people have contributed, both directly and indirectly, to the topic, format, initial composition, revision, and mechanical production of the manuscript that eventually became this book. They cannot possibly all be acknowledged. Special mention, however, should be made of Professors Constantin V. Boundas, John W. Burbidge, Robert E. Carter, Bernard J. Hodgson, and M. Lionel Rubinoff, all of Trent University, who provided me with friendly criticisms and suggestions, both while the lectures were in process of presentation and in subsequent discussions. I should also like to thank Professor Edward Casey, Chair of the Department of Philosophy at the State University of New York at Stony Brook, for arranging a series of lectures and intensive seminars in April 1995 in which certain themes in this book were developed further. The comments and recommendations by Professor Casey and members of his philosophy faculty and graduate students at Stony Brook were particularly helpful in preparing the manuscript for publication. Professor Martin C. Dillon of the State University of New York at Binghamton provided a rigorous and detailed critical evaluation of the penultimate draft of the manuscript. Without his pointed and penetrating assessment, numerous miscues would have remained unattended to. I must quickly add, however, that those who have offered their advice and helpful suggestions should in no way be held responsible for the imperfections that remain in the text.

In conclusion, I wish to express my thanks to Stephen Pluháĉek for his help in correcting proof and drawing up the index. And I certainly would be remiss would I fail to acknowledge the technical competence, persistence, and patience of Pamela Connelly, whose mastery of cyberspace facilitated the movement of the manuscript through its sundry revisions to its final disposition.

INTRODUCTION

The project of sketching the portrait of the human self after postmodernity invites difficulties that many may deem insurmountable. There is first the obvious truth that we are dealing not with a single, unitary, sharply defined portrait, but rather with a portrait that is itself curiously diversified. What thus appears to be at issue is a multiplicity of profiles and perspectives through which the human self moves and is able to come into view. The insinuation of diversity and multiplicity across the spectrum of human affairs is indeed something that we have learned from our postmodern experience and that itself needs to become a topic for discussion.

There is, however, another set of obstacles facing the projected undertaking. This has to do with the very grammar of portraits or profiles or perspectives. It is a grammar that invites a philosophical optics bent upon the field of vision as somehow privileged for the disclosure of self and world. But knowledge of self is as much the rendering of an account, the telling of a story, as it is the discernment of perceptual profiles—and indeed it is the telling of a story in which the self is announced as at once actor and receiver of action. It is this integration and entwinement of seeing, storytelling, and acting that needs to be underscored. I thus propose a metaphorical extension of the grammar of portraits, profiles, or perspectives to include the telling and hearing of stories and the performance and reception of action.

In delineating portraits, composing narratives, or providing accounts of human action, one always finds it difficult to decide how to begin. Perplexity becomes intensified when one realizes that there are no necessary starting points. All starting points are contingent. One could always choose another beginning. And the quandary of this peculiar predicament is further compounded by the realization that in a consequential sense one is always already begun, situated in medias res, as it were, searching for an entry into a conversation and a positioning in a state of affairs that is always already on its way.

Consequently one is required to become attuned to the discussions already in progress, and one would do well to begin addressing the selected topic by focusing on a commonly rehearsed motif in the literature of postmodernity. This motif has taken on a variety of formulations, to wit the "death of man," the "death of the author," the "deconstruction of the subject," the "displacement of the ego," the "dissolution of self-identity," and at times a combination of all the above. Michel Foucault had already publicized the death of man in one of his early writings, in which the reader is informed that "man is an invention of recent date" and will soon "be erased like a face drawn in the sand at the edge of the sea."[1] This missive pertaining to the demise of man as a philosophically useful concept is to be understood, according to Foucault, as the proper sequel to Friedrich Nietzsche's earlier proclamation of the death of God. In dismantling the concept of God as a metaphysical aberration Nietzsche prepared the way for a similar fate befalling the concept of man.

Roughly at the same time as Foucault's announcement of the death of man, his compatriot Roland Barthes exploited the newly articulated motif in the arena of literary studies by composing a requiem for the author. The Barthian litany on the death of the author was designed to dethrone the sovereignty of

---

1. Michel Foucault, *The Order of Things: An Archaeology of the Human Sciences* (New York: Random House, 1970), p. 387.

the author in matters of textual meaning and to expunge once and for all the "intentional fallacy," which over the years had skewed both literary and philosophical studies. Soon to follow was the widely circulated and vigorously discussed requirement set forth by Jacques Derrida for a deconstruction of the subject, which has achieved the proverbial household familiarity. Confronted with the mosaic of messages dealing with the death of man, the demise of the author, and the deconstruction or dissimulation of the subject, one finds oneself in a crisis of concepts relative to matters pertaining to the human self understood as subject and agent in discourse and action.

Although the vocabularies employed in the traditional descriptions and definitions of the human self—such as substance and attribute, form and matter, subject, mind, ego, and self-identity—have been singled out for sustained attack in the postmodern era, these vocabularies had already come under criticism by certain proponents of modernity. What needs to be recognized is that the issue at stake in these apparently interminable discussions and critiques is long-standing and perhaps inescapable, extending back to ancient Greece, where it was given a poignant expression in the Socratic requirement for the achievement of self-knowledge. Socrates' existential imperative "Know thyself!" and its direct corollary "The unexamined life is not worth living" may indeed confront us with obligations that are as pertinent today as they were for the ancients. It should be remembered, however, that the installation of the Socratic requirement for the achievement of self-knowledge occurred in advance of the accelerated and often feverish metaphysical speculation that followed in its wake.

Gilbert Ryle, in developing his ordinary language approach to philosophical issues, provided the Socratic requirement with a contemporary expression, bringing into question the bold application of metaphysical categories in the pursuit of self-knowledge. More specifically, the lasting contribution of Ryle's philosophical endeavors was a dismantling of the Cartesian portrait of the human subject as an interiorized mental substance. The explorations that follow reflect, albeit in a somewhat oblique manner, the abiding inspiration of Ryle's philosophy. In these explorations I attempt to continue some of the critical discussions that he initiated.

The binding textuality of the successive chapters trades on the historical concepts of psyche, self, mind, ego, and subject. These concepts, because of their accumulation of extraneous vocabularies in their long histories, need to become topics for critical interrogation, a requirement that has become intensified in the aftermath of the shattering indictments of the grammars of subjectivity and selfhood by a variety of postmodern thinkers. My intention is to refigure and retrench the question about the self through a shift of grammar as I examine the more notable profiles of self-presentation. Framing the discussion in terms of "who" questions instead of "what" questions, I shall conduct explorations of the self in discourse, the self in action, the self in community, and the self in transcendence against the backdrop of such inquiries as "Who is speaking?" "Who is acting?" "Who responds to other selves?" and "Who stands within and before transcendence?" Although I shall not jettison the vocabularies of the "subject" and "subjectivity," I shall make an effort to keep these vocabularies contextualized within the density of a concrete "who experience," the traces of which are most visible in the pursuit of issues pertaining to the who of our quotidian and lived-through communicative practices of speaking, listening, narrating, acting, working, and playing.

The principal profiles or features or perspectives in the following portrait of the self—the self in discourse, the self in action, the self in community, and the self in transcendence—intersect a complementing configuration of formative factors that enter into the constitution of what we are wont to call the human self. This complementing configuration illustrates the cultural achievements of the human subject throughout its historical development, including advances in the domains of science, morality, art, and religion. These domains comprise the configurations of human experience that are generally referenced in the literature as the "culture-spheres" of modernity. Attentiveness to the role of these culture-spheres is necessary to avoid portraying the human self in isolation from its cultural contexts, as a self abstracted from the concretion of its historical development.

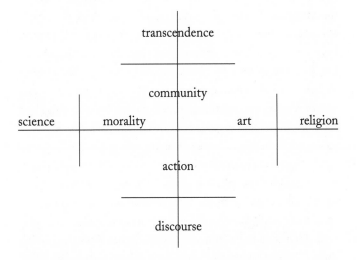

The format of the envisioned portrait follows the lines and directions of a diagrammatic mapping, using the spatial metaphors of verticality and horizontality, picturing the profiles of discourse, action, community, and transcendence as ingredients of a synchronics of self-understanding and the culture-spheres of science, morality, art, and religion as the moving figures within a diachronics of historical constitution. In rendering an account of the human self, one must keep in mind that at every juncture, as it were, the synchronics of self-understanding and the diachronics of historico-cultural constitution intersect, reinforce one another, and stand in a relation of complementarity.

In pursuing the themes that fall out from the complementarity of self-understanding and historico-cultural constitution, we will need to coordinate the concreteness of the "who" within the projects of speaking and acting with the historical forms that have a hand in the shaping of our ends, working behind our backs as we seek to understand the selves that we are. Of these historical forces and configurations of self and social formation, science, morality, and art have received particular attention in the literature. Indeed, the principal interpreters of the development of modernity, from Max Weber to Jürgen Habermas, have veritably defined modernity as the differentiation of culture into the spheres of science, morality, and art. What both Weber and Habermas may have overlooked is the contribution of religion as a legitimate fourth culture-sphere of modern thought. In the fourth chapter of this book, "The Self in Transcendence," the consequence of such an oversight is addressed.

The definition of modernity, as framed by Weber and Habermas, highlights the splitting apart ("stubborn differentiation" is what Weber called it) of the three domains of science, morality, and art. The culprit behind this unhappy differentiation is generally identified to be Immanuel Kant. It was Kant who, in his three *Critiques,* marked off the boundaries of science, morality, and art in such a wise as to render any unification of the three spheres highly problematic, if not impossible. G. W. F. Hegel took up the gauntlet, but according to his more reliable critics he failed. His project of a dialectical mediation of opposites fell short of the unification that he envisioned. The distinguished company that composed the School of anti-Hegelians —Ludwig Feuerbach, Søren Kierkegaard, and Karl Marx—

achieved considerable recognition by calling the world's attention to the failures of Hegelianism. With a combination of maieutic irony and penetrating insight they recognized that the unity of the rational and the real, and the identity of essence and existence, projected as the culmination of Hegel's "System," was an *abstract* unity and identity, localized in Hegel's head, never making its way into the concrete concerns that pervade the sensory-biological, ethico-religious, and socioeconomic spheres of human life.

Habermas's position on the role of Hegel in the narrative of modernity is singular. He is of the mind that Hegel had a proper understanding of the requirement—namely, that of unifying the three culture-spheres—and that he got off to a promising start with his early writings but then messed things up quite badly in his later works when he began to make claims for an absolute knowledge grounded in a subject-centered rationality. Habermas's project is that of redirecting the wrong turn taken by the later Hegel and solving the problem of the fragmented culture-spheres with a doctrine of communicative rationality that is centered on processes of societal formation rather than on an abstracted subject.

In the current discussions of the issue there are those who are of the opinion that the very "problem of modernity" is contrived rather than genuine. We call these "postmodernists," and they come in many different forms. They seem to agree, however, that the need to unify the culture-spheres, as proposed by Hegel and Habermas, is not a genuine need. Indeed, the grammars of unity, totality, identity, sameness, and consensus find little employment in postmodern thinking. Jean-François Lyotard, putatively the chief voice of the current postmodernists, makes this quite clear when he announces in his postmodern manifesto that "consensus does violence to the heterogeneity of language games" and that we need to "tolerate the incommensurable," "wage a war on totality," and "activate the differences."[2] Heterogeneity, multiplicity, diversity, difference, incommensurability, and dissensus become the chief interpretive categories of the postmodern mind. Insofar as the function of reason was defined in the thought of both the ancients and the moderns as a drive toward the totalization and unification of human experience, the stance of postmodernity becomes that of *other than reason.*

The consequences of this stance for an understanding of the self or the human subject are considerable. For the most part, questions about the self, and particularly questions about the self *as subject,* are deemed anathema. As there is no longer a need for the unification of the diverse culture-spheres, so the problem of the self, at least as traditionally formulated, is seen to evaporate. Questions about self-identity, the unity of consciousness, and centralized and goal-directed activity have been displaced in the aftermath of the dissolution of the subject. If one cannot rid oneself of the vocabulary of self, subject, and mind, the most that can be asserted is that the self is multiplicity, heterogeneity, difference, and ceaseless becoming, bereft of origin and purpose. Such is the manifesto of postmodernity on matters of the human subject as self and mind.

The succeeding chapters have been designed to respond to this formidable challenge by the architects of postmodernity. In them an effort is made to resituate and refigure the portrait of the human self after its traditional metaphysical supports and epistemological guarantees have been called into question. Although agreeing with the postmodernists in their assaults on both the classical substance-theory of the self and the modern

2. Jean-François Lyotard, *The Postmodern Condition: A Report on Knowledge,* trans. Geoff Bennington and Brian Massumi (Minneapolis: University of Minnesota Press, 1984), pp. xxv, 82.

epistemological or foundationalist construal of self as transparent mind, the principal argument is that a jettisoning of the self understood in these senses does not entail a jettisoning of every sense of self. In the aftermath of the deconstruction of traditional metaphysics and epistemology, a new self emerges, like the phoenix arising from its ashes—a praxis-oriented self, defined by its communicative practices, oriented toward an understanding of itself in its discourse, its action, its being with others, and its experience of transcendence. The narration of this story of self-understanding is scripted as a response both to the discourse of modernity and to the postmodern challenge, addressing the roles of the culture-spheres of science, morality, art, and religion in their functions of defining the sociohistorical process of self-formation.

I

The Self in Discourse

Gilbert Ryle opens his classic and widely influential work *The Concept of Mind* with a statement of what he calls the "official doctrine" on the distinction between mind and body in the annals of modern philosophy. Human bodies exist in space, are open to inspection by external observers, and are subject to the laws of mechanics that govern the movements of physical objects. Human minds, in contrast, are not in space, are known through introspection rather than by observation, and are exempt from models of mechanistic explanation. Human bodies are public, and the events that they exhibit are external; the career of mind is private, and the events that compose its workings are internal. It is thus that the official doctrine delivers a dualism—a dualism of body versus mind, the public versus the private, the external versus the internal, and the mechanistic versus the vitalistic.[1]

Even the philosophical novice will recognize this formulation of the dualism of body and mind to be the invention of the father of modern philosophy, René Descartes. And the portrait of mind peculiar to the Cartesian legacy, as piquantly expressed by Ryle, is that of a mythical ghost in the machine. Ryle's project in *The Concept of Mind* is to dispel this myth—or, in more contemporary parlance, to *deconstruct* it, dismantle it in such a manner that it is seen to rest on a category-mistake, a

1. Gilbert Ryle, *The Concept of Mind* (New York: Barnes and Noble, 1949), pp. 11–12.

representation of mental events as belonging to one logical type when in fact they belong to another.

One might express solid agreement with Ryle's dissatisfaction with Cartesian dualism, which as he points out has left its mark on the philosophy of modernity generally, and yet enter the discussion at another level or juncture, possibly in such a manner that a more originative insight on the part of Descartes might be salvaged and a conversation with him continued. This would involve a species of deconstruction of our own—to wit, a dismantling of Descartes's proclivity to approach the problem of selfhood with a "what" question by reformulating it into a "who" question.

An anecdote involving the pedagogical skills of the late American philosopher Morris Cohen illustrates the point at issue. As the story goes, Cohen had in his course on modern philosophy a student of profound seriousness, intent on finding truths that are unassailable and unimpeachable. It was thus that Cohen's lecture on Descartes's argument for the indubitability of the cogito, with its pungent concluding declaration "I think, therefore I am," quickened the student's spirit. Finally, a bedrock truth! Yet, being of questioning temperament, the student soon found problems with Descartes's argument—and the more problems he found, the more perplexed he became. How could he be *absolutely sure* that even he existed? After some days of anxiety-ridden wrestling with the question, on the verge of despair, he pleadingly approached his mentor, "Professor, *do I exist?*"—to which Cohen wryly responded, "Who wants to know?"

There is in this anecdote, whether factual or apocryphal, both a display of levity and a measure of philosophical weight. Of particular interest in Cohen's response is a shift in the hermeneutics of inquiry, deconstructing the Cartesian "what" question down to a "who" question. Descartes was in search of an answer to the question "What is the self?"—he was calling for the specification of a *nature* or an *essence*. As even the proverbial "every schoolboy" knows, Descartes allegedly found this nature or essence to be that of a thinking or mental substance, a *res cogitans*, a thing that thinks, a residuum that remains in the wake of the exercise of a rigorous methodological procedure of systematic doubt that is to leave no stone unturned. But subsequent inquiry showed, as the hapless student in Cohen's class apparently surmised, that the definition of the self as a mental substance remains forever undecidable, perpetually deferred, destined to become a vacuous concept.

But the dismantling of the epistemological foundation and metaphysical support of an underlying mental substance does not of necessity bring to a halt all inquires about the human self. It may simply indicate the need for a change of perspective, a refiguration of our mode of questioning, putting us in quest not of an abstract universal nature but rather of a concrete and historically specific questioner. The question about the who thus becomes a question about the questioner. Gary B. Madison is on target when he reproaches the architects of modernity for having framed the question about the human subject "metaphysically, in terms of natures and essence" and then "proceeded to translate the existential question 'Who am I?' into the metaphysical question, 'What is man?'"[2]

The central point at issue is highlighted in the choice of the title for the collection of essays and interviews *Who Comes after the Subject?* After the subject as metaphysically defined nature or essence has been disassembled, the requirement for a retrieval of the who of discourse and the who of action would appear to remain in force. This collection of essays and interviews has a

2. Gary B. Madison, *The Hermeneutics of Postmodernity: Figures and Themes* (Bloomington: Indiana University Press, 1988), p. 155.

quite direct bearing on the current project of telling the story of self after postmodernity because it gives voice to some of the household names in the pantheon of postmodernists. The response Jacques Derrida gives to Jean-Luc Nancy's query "Who comes after the subject?" is of particular moment: "What are we aiming at in the deconstructions of the 'subject' when we ask ourselves what, in the structure of the classical subject, continues to be required by the question 'Who?' . . . . I would add something that remains required by both the definitions of the classical subject and by these later nonclassical motifs, namely a certain responsibility. The singularity of the 'who' is not the individuality of a thing that would be identical with itself, it is not an atom. It is a singularity that dislocates or divides itself in gathering itself together to answer to the other, whose call somehow precedes its own identification with itself."[3]

3. Eduardo Cadava, Peter Connor, and Jean-Luc Nancy, eds., *Who Comes after the Subject?* (New York: Routledge, 1991), p. 100.   Derrida's reply to Nancy's query recalls an exchange that took place in 1966 at the much publicized Johns Hopkins International Colloquium on the Human Sciences. Serge Doubrovsky pressed Derrida on the fate of the subject consequent to its deconstruction, and Derrida replied: "I don't destroy the subject. I situate it. That is to say, I believe that at a certain level both of experience and scientific discourse one cannot get along without the notion of the subject. It is a question of knowing where it comes from and how it functions" (*The Languages of Criticism and the Sciences of Man: The Structuralist Controversy,* ed. Richard Macksey and Eugenio Donato [Baltimore: John Hopkins University Press, 1970, p. 271]). There is clearly a story within a story in this transition or shift from the Derrida of 1966 to the Derrida of 1986, which would seem to have much to do with his move from a confrontation with structuralism to his discovery or rediscovery of Emmanuel Levinas. The grammar of responsibility, which guides Derrida's response to Nancy, has a heavy Levinasian undertow. But what requires notice is that the question about the subject retains its pertinence throughout the different stages of its deconstruction. To be sure, the question itself takes on different formulations as it proceeds from context to context, but the *Sache* at stake in the questioning remains intact.

The question about the who, is not, as Derrida correctly remarks, an inquiry into the "individuality of a thing" but is rather, as Cohen's student came to realize, an existentially motivated question about the questioner. Who is asking the question about her or his existence? And might one even be able to grant to Descartes, the accomplished master of scientifically oriented methodological doubt, the benefit of the doubt that he too was motivated by a more existentially oriented concern about the who of Descartes as author of the *Discourse* and the *Meditations* and about the who of Descartes as actor in the world of public affairs? It is revealing to compare Descartes's formal philosophical writings with his informal and decidedly more personal letters and note differences in both style and content. His philosophical treatises are couched in the technical grammar of metaphysics and theory of knowledge. His letters exhibit the grammar of ordinary language and deal with matters of proximate existential concerns.

Such is particularly the case with his letters written to Father Mersenne and Princess Elizabeth, in which the discourse turns on various bodily ailments and possible medical cures. One can detect in these letters a drift away from the official doctrine on the mind-body dualism as it was formulated in *Meditation* VI. Discourse about the mind and the body becomes palpably concretized in these letters, and especially in the one that he wrote to Princess Elizabeth addressing the problem of her somewhat mysterious fever. She had been suffering for several weeks, and all efforts to locate a purely somatic origin came up short. This prompted Descartes to surmise that Elizabeth's fever had as a contributing factor a certain condition of melancholy or sadness of the soul, suggesting that the relation of the mind and body is more of a concrete interrelation than a juxtaposition of two substances. So not only does the shift from Descartes's technical philosophical treatises to his informal letters tell us something about the difference of discursive styles, it also tells us something about the difference between viewing the self as an entity for epistemological and metaphysical speculation and viewing it as a who that is inserted into the density of concrete life experiences.[4] From this one might extract a more general guideline for Descartes scholarship, recommending that his philosophical treatises be cross-read with his personal correspondence.

The task of this chapter is to examine the formation process of the self as a who that is implicated in the economy of discourse. We speak of discourse as an economy because it involves a production and consumption, a distribution and exchange, of speech and language, a display of the dynamics of the word as spoken and the word as written. Ferdinand de Saussure's distinction between speech and language, *parole* and *langue,* is surely a useful one, but one must stand guard against its reification into a bogus dichotomy of empirical speech acts and language as a system of signs, against the separation of a phenomenology of speaking from a semiotics of meaning. Speech acts and linguistic systems, speaking and meaning, are closely intertextured. The self that speaks, the speaking subject, is already involved in the production of meaning as it distributes and exchanges signs that are part of the structure of language as a system. Speaking is a creative act, at once a discovery of self and a self-constitution, but a creative act that takes place only against the background of a language already spoken, which has both a history and a formal structure, a language ensconced in the tradition, operating behind our backs, as Hans-Georg Gadamer would be wont to say. Discourse is the symbiotic event of an intercalation of speaking with a language

4. For a discussion of Descartes in the role of medical consultant in his various letters see Richard Zaner's perceptive analysis in his book *Ethics and the Clinical Encounter* (Englewood Cliffs, N.J.: Prentice Hall, 1988), pp. 108–116.

from which one speaks. When we speak, we speak a language, and thus we always speak *from* a language, from a context of delivered significations. Words, whether spoken or written, live off the capital of language, albeit in different ways, and stimulate the economy of discourse as at once a creative achievement and a deliverance of meanings already uttered, at once event and system, at once articulation of that which is new and repetition of that which is old.

It is within this economy of discourse that the self is called into being, and it is called into being as the who that is speaking and listening, writing and reading, discursing in a variety of situations and modalities of discourse. In a previous work, I articulated this recognition of the self in its discourse as an adventure of "hermeneutical self-implicature."[5] The self is implicated in its discourse as a who that at the crossroads of speech and language understands itself as a self that has already spoken, is now speaking, and has the power yet to speak, suspended across the temporal dimensions of past, present, and future. In this temporalized economy of discourse the self lives through a multiplicity of changing profiles and a plurality of language games in which it holds court, but not without some sense of self-identity—some sense of the same self being present to itself in its remembered past, its engaged present, and its projected future.

But how is one to articulate and illustrate this sense of self-identity amid the multiplicity and flux of our forms of discourse and language games? It is surely a fair historical observation that philosophy in the twentieth century has been much preoccupied with discourse and language. The epithet "the lin-

5. See Calvin O. Schrag, *Communicative Praxis and the Space of Subjectivity* (Bloomington: Indiana University Press, 1986), chap. 6, "Hermeneutical Self-Implicature," pp. 115-138.

guistic turn in philosophy" has often been used to characterize Anglo-American and continental philosophy alike. Ludwig
Wittgenstein's later writings, emphasizing the role of language
in marking out various "forms of life," had much to do with
this, as did the contributions of Ryle and J. L. Austin in charting the program of ordinary language philosophy. On the Continent, Gadamer worked out a project of ontological hermeneutics at mid-century culminating in his magnum opus, *Truth and
Method*, with its influential "linguisticality of being" doctrine.
Jean-François Lyotard, consolidating his theses on postmodernism, bounced off Wittgenstein's notion of language games
and developed an elaborate treatise called *The Differend*, celebrating the heterogeneity in the usage of language against the
backdrop of a "rhetorical agonistics" that projects the goal of
discourse to be conflict and disagreement instead of dialogue
oriented toward consensus.[6] Jürgen Habermas undertook what
may be the boldest project of all, namely, that of integrating
a theory of speech acts into his massive two-volume work *The
Theory of Communicative Action*. His threefold division of validity claims (truth of propositions, rightness of normative obli-

6. Jean-François Lyotard, *The Differend: Phrases in Dispute*, trans.
George Van Den Abbeele (Minneapolis: University of Minnesota Press,
1988), p. 26. Lyotard's project of a postmodern rhetoric, flagged as a "rhetorical agonistics," proceeds from his distinction between the "partisans of
agonistics" and the "partisans of dialogue." The first are able to activate
the differend in recognition that there are no common referents in our
heterogenous language games and that the striving for consensus on the
part of the partisans of dialogue is based on an illusory ideal. See also
Lyotard's criticism of Habermas in *The Postmodern Condition*, where he
disputes Habermas's claim that the goal of dialogue is consensus with
the rejoinder that "consensus is only a particular state of discussion, not
its end. Its end, on the contrary, is paralogy" (trans. Geoff Bennington
and Brian Massumi [Minneapolis: University of Minnesota Press, 1984],
p. 65–66).

gations, and authenticity of self-disclosure) through which the culture-spheres of science, morality, and art receive their articulation is correlated with a corresponding threefold division of speech acts, including the constative or denotative function, the regulative function, and the expressive function.

In all these developments the role of discourse, as an amalgam of speech and language, has come into prominence, and clearly these developments are directly relevant to our current task of seeking to locate the self within the interstices of discourse. The first profile in the portrait of the self to be examined is that of the self constituting itself as it lives in and through a maze of speech acts and a plethora of language games, articulating its thoughts and expressing its feelings within the spheres of scientific, moral, artistic, and religious endeavors. Coupled with this first profile is the claim that such a process of self-formation is made possible by the resources of discourse itself. This is not to say that no factors other than discourse are involved in the process of self-formation. Indeed, in the succeeding chapters these other factors will be addressed, but the point to be made at this juncture is that in dealing with the issue of self-identity within the economy of discourse there is no need for an appeal either to a changeless underlying substratum or to an epistemic Archimedean point to account for the unity and self-identity of the who of discourse. Discourse provides its own resources for self-unification and self-identity, and it does so specifically in the form and dynamics of narrative.

The introduction of narrative constitutes a critical supplementary perspective in any account of the who of discourse. Narrative provides the ongoing context in which the figures of discourse are embedded and achieve their determinations of sense and reference. Narrative supplies the horizon of possible meanings that stimulate the economy of discourse. Some of these meanings have been articulated in stories already told;

others are potential meanings yet to be unfolded in the emplotment of future narratives. The horizon of narrativity thus suffers a temporal imprinting, emerging from a past and advancing into a future, recollective of stories that have become part of a tradition and anticipative of accounts, both fictive and factual, yet to be rendered. Narrative comprises the continuing context, the expanding horizon of a retentional background and a protentional foreground, in which and against which our figures of discourse are called into being, play themselves out, and conspire in the making of sense.

Without the contextualizing of discourse in the configurations of narrative, discourse stands in danger of being pulverized into abstracted, atomistic, static, elemental units. In such a reduction to elemental units, the figures of discourse are shorn of all intentionality, all vectors of sense, and all illustrations of reference. In understanding discourse as a creative event of articulation it is necessary to emphasize the entwinement and interplay of speech and language so as to avoid any empiricistic reduction of speaking to isolated "speech acts" and any accompanying semiotic reduction of language to its abstracted phonemic, morphemic, and lexical elements. In the move to narrative we proceed to another level and a broader context in which the figures of discourse as amalgams of speech and language produce and exchange meanings.

The proper placement of discourse vis-à-vis its alliance with speech and language on the one hand and narrativity on the other hand can be illustrated via a mapping in which discourse is located "between" the constitutive elements of speech and language and the wider contextual and holistic intertexture of narratives. The point that needs to be stressed in this mapping of interconnections is that the critical zone in which the who is called into being is the zone of the discursive event. The question about the who has minimal relevance in a science of

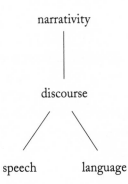

narrativity

|

discourse

/ \

speech   language

linguistics, oriented as it is toward an analysis and explanation of lexical and sublexical constitutive elements. Questions about the origin and the status of the who simply do not arise on the level of lexicography, syntactics, morphology, and phonemics. Linguistic science, as a science, progresses independently of any psychological, epistemological, or existential interest in the fortunes and misfortunes of a self or subject. It simply abstracts away from questions and interests of this sort. Likewise, an empirical inquiry into speech acts decontextualizes the event of speaking so as to objectify the constitutive features of speech— physiological, psychological, and ethnographic. In such an inquiry, as in that of linguistic science, the question about the who has little bearing on the investigative procedures. It is only when one moves to the level of the discursive event, in which there is an effort to communicate something about something to someone, that the question "Who is speaking?" takes on relevance and indeed becomes uncircumventable.

Now, the who that is announced on the level of discourse is already a participant in and a respondent to the narratives that have shaped the tradition and those that envision future developments of self and society. It is in this sense that narrativity provides the wider horizon for the constitution of discursive meaning. The internal connection between discourse and its narratival horizon and background must be maintained. If discourse loses its contextual horizon of narrative, then the achievement of meaning through the articulatory resources of discourse is threatened. If, in contrast, narrative is cut loose from discourse, from the event of speaking as someone saying something to someone, then the who that is speaking is destined for displacement.

The severing of narrative from discourse is precisely the inherent danger in the uses of narrative in the constructive designs of *narratology*. Narratology, in its striving to become a rigorous semiotic science of narrative, transforms narrative into an object of disinterested scientific inquiry, abstracts away from the temporality of discursive experience, and reifies narrative as a veritable deus ex machina. Insofar as temporality becomes an issue for narratology, it functions as a cinematographic image or simulacrum of the time that informs and invigorates the transmission of stories already shared and the anticipation of stories yet to be told. This construct of temporality in narratology ends up as an *atemporal* structure that intrudes like a blade, severing narrative temporality from its sources in the concrete temporalization of events of discourse. In short, narratology ruptures, tears asunder, narrative and discourse. Within such a scheme of things the who has no voice. The who of discourse is swallowed by an abstract mechanics of narratival form and function. Narratology is a representation of narrative without a narrator.

Therefore we must stand guard to secure the space of discourse as temporalized event of speaking *between* the objectification of speech acts and language on the one hand and the abstractions and reifications in the structuralist designs of narratology on the other hand. The event of discourse as a saying of something by someone to someone is threatened from both "below" and "above"—from below in terms of a tendency toward an ontology of elementarism fixated on the isolable, constitutive elements of speech acts and linguistic units (phonemes, morphemes, lexemes), and from above in the sense of a predilection toward an abstract holism of narratological structures that leaves the event of discourse behind. Only by sticking to the terrain of the "between" will the subject as the who of discourse and the who of narrative remain visible. It is on this terrain, which we will later come to call the terrain of lived-experience, that we are able to observe the august event of a self understanding itself through the twin moments of discourse and narration.

The explicit linkage of narrative to an understanding of self and world has already received a hearing in the burgeoning literature on the topic. Mark Johnson, in his well-received book *Moral Imagination: Implications of Cognitive Science for Ethics*, puts the relation of narrative and understanding in its proper perspective when he writes, "There are various types of narrative structures that play a role in how we understand actions, evaluate moral character, and project possible solutions to morally problematic situations. *Narrative is not just an explanatory device, but is actually constitutive of the way we experience things*" (emphasis mine).[7]

Johnson's accentuation of the role of understanding within the economy of narrative is given a strong endorsement in Donald E. Polkinghorne's influential study *Narrative Knowing and the Human Sciences*. Polkinghorne defines and explicates narrative as a "form of 'meaning making'" that organizes human experience into meaningful episodes, functioning as a "lens through which the apparently independent and disconnected elements of existence are seen as related parts of a

7. Mark Johnson, *Moral Imagination: Implications of Cognitive Science for Ethics* (Chicago: University of Chicago Press, 1993), p. 11.

whole."[8] In this function, narrative plays a *cognitive* role. Cognition according to Polkinghorne, however, is neither decontextualized objectification and explanation of isolated empirical and linguistic data nor abstract structural schematization. Cognition unfolds as a pre-objective understanding of self and world within discursive practices. Admittedly, there is a holism at work in the dynamics of narrative cognition, keeping at bay the elementarism of empiricistic and semiotic reductionism, but it is not the abstract holism of a narratology bent upon explanation via structures of textuality. As a practicing psychotherapist, Polkinghorne is profoundly interested in the implications of narrative knowing and understanding for the theory and practice of psychotherapy. Seeing a direct relevance of narrative for psychotherapy and for the agenda of the human sciences more generally, he emphasizes the "importance of research strategies that can work with the narratives people use to understand the human world."[9]

The role of narrative in its function of knowing and understanding, which both Johnson and Polkinghorne have helped us bring into prominence, has a direct bearing on our project of devising a new portrait of the self, relating specifically to the issue of the status of the who of discourse and the problem of self-identity. The who of discourse as a narrating self, articulating both proximate and remote concerns, understands itself in its hearing and transmitting of narratives. It is of particular consequence to underscore that the cognition at issue, with its vectors of self-knowledge and knowledge of the world, is limned by the narratival context and background. We need to recall time and again the enriched notion of cognition at work

8. Donald E. Polkinghorne, *Narrative Knowing and the Human Sciences* (Albany: State University of New York Press, 1988), p. 36.

9. *Narrative Knowing and the Human Sciences*, p. xi.

in narrative understanding, which both Johnson and Polking-horne have highlighted in their studies. No longer at issue is the classical modernist construal of cognition as proceeding from a translucent cogito struggling to apprehend itself and the variegated furniture of the universe as unblemished *cogitata,* oriented toward a theoretical grounding of all knowledge in a foundationalist epistemology. Such an epistemological or foundationalist construal of knowledge needs to be delimited, if not indeed more radically problematized.

The foundationalist paradigm proffers a theoretical construct of mind that is designed to determine in advance the criteria for what counts as knowledge, both knowledge of oneself and knowledge of the world. It is as though one were required to know how to swim before one swims, or to know grammatical rules of language before one knows how to speak, or to master the criteria for proper etiquette before knowing how to function in society. But to say that one knows before one knows — or indeed to say that one not only knows but knows *that* one knows, activating the *logos* of *epistēmē* — would seem to catapult the very project of epistemology into a species of philosophical circularity if not indeed philosophical incoherence.

Surely a lesson to be learned from the challenge mounted by postmodernity is that modernity's invention of mind as a transparent mental mirror, and the accompanying invention of a theoretico-epistemological paradigm that legislates criteria in advance, contributed little to an understanding of the human self in its manifold concretion as speaking and narrating subject. The modern concepts of mind and knowledge conspired in the construction of an abstracted, insular knowing subject, severed from the context and contingencies out of which knowledge of self and knowledge of the world arise. The subject as abstracted epistemological pivot, as atemporal zero-point origin of cognition, is wrested from the lived-experiences of a speaking and narrating self that always already understands itself in its speech and in its narration. Knowledge contextualized and informed by narratives that transmit a tradition and anticipate and pre-enact a future is older than the decontextualized analyses of abstracted conditions for knowledge and the objectified data of human behavior. This does not as such invalidate claims for decontextualized and objectified information about elemental units by linguistic analysis or about methodologically controlled data in the several human sciences, but it does liberate us from the myriad temptations of a reductionism that envisions a knowledge of self and world independent of context.

Such a required context has been found in the dynamics of narrative. In this move to narrativity, however, one must be duly vigilant about another danger on the path toward self-understanding, namely, the solidification of narrative into a narratology that disconnects itself from the concrete temporality of the who of discourse. To avoid this danger one should pay particular attention to the explicit entwinement of the event of discourse with the telling of narratives. Narratives need to be told by someone to someone. If narrative does not tell a story to someone, then it is not narrative; if discourse is not a rendition by someone, then it is not discourse. This accounts for the concretion of narrative in the events of speaking and writing.

We have now arrived at the self's understanding of itself at the crossroads of discourse and narration as a who of discourse in the guise of a narrating self, a *homo narrans*, a storyteller who both finds herself in stories already told and strives for a self-constitution by emplotting herself in stories in the making. To be a self is to be able to render an account of oneself, to be able to tell the story of one's life. Sometimes we are at the mercy of the stories that we tell, and at other times the stories suffer the inscription of our own agenda. One might speak of such a self as *emergent*, a self emerging from the panoply of communicative practices in which it always already finds itself implicated, an accomplice in the utterances of speech acts and in the significations of language. This recognition of the self as emergent from and implicated by the variegated forms of discourse provides a sheet anchor against recurring tendencies to construct a sovereign and monarchical self, at once self-sufficient and self-assured, finding metaphysical comfort in a doctrine of an immutable and indivisible self-identity. Such a doctrine has become a prime target for the protagonists of postmodernism.

Chief among the features and defining marks of postmodernity, both as a philosophical perspective and as a cultural expression, is a celebration of difference and diversity. In the arena of discourse this celebration highlights the plurality and multiplicity of our forms of speech and our language games. Lyotard's version of postmodernism pretty much rests on his claim for a "heterogeneity of language games." This heterogeneity is not only the occasion for splitting off scientific knowledge from narrative knowledge, but also the basis for separating denotative, deontic, normative, ablative, interrogative, and emotive genres into isolated enclaves. Within such an economy of discourse it is indeed difficult to find traces of a unified self, much less a self-identical subject. The self is simply dispersed into a panorama of radically diversified and changing language games. If indeed the grammar of "self" continues to be employed, it would need to be said that it is in each case a different self that makes assertoric claims, evaluations, moral judgments, inquiries, aesthetic judgments, and emotive utterances.

Although Lyotard's contributions toward framing the postmodern challenge have indeed been considerable and have enabled us to learn a considerable amount about the vagaries in the veneration of unity, totality, and identity by the voices of modernity, it would appear that in the proverbial final analysis the postmodern counteractant of celebrating plurality, incompleteness, and difference may well be an overreaction that leaves us with a subject too thin to bear the responsibilities of its narratival involvements. Hence, our project takes the direction of an inquiry toward the portrait of the self as subject *after* postmodernity. After all the postmodern dust has settled, what traces remain of the self in discourse, the self in action, the self in community, and the self in transcendence?

In seeking to sketch a refigured portrait of the self in discourse, we need to give particular attention to the postmodern challenge as it relates to the problematization of all claims for a unity and self-identity of the discursive and narrational self. And it is Lyotard, clearly the most postmodern of the postmodernists, who leads the charge in the frontal assault on philosophies of unity and identity. Lyotard's arsenal is drawn principally from the linguistic philosophy of Wittgenstein, whose influence he readily acknowledges. He formulates his doctrine of the heterogeneity of language games against the backdrop of Wittgenstein's analysis of meaning as residing in linguistic usages. As for Wittgenstein the usage (and hence meaning) of language is multiple, so for Lyotard language games illustrate a multiplicity of forms and functions — constative, deontic, normative, prescriptive, interrogative, expressive — and there appears to be little if any connection among them. Hence, to speak even of a linguistic subject or self is problematic, for there is no unifying thread that extends transversally across the multiple functions. Thus, not only are language games multiple, they are also heterogeneous.[10]

10. Although Lyotard acknowledges his debt to Wittgenstein, as well as to John Searle and the Anglo-American School of Linguistic Analysis more generally, there may be some problems with Lyotard's postmodern reading of Wittgenstein in particular. There is no doubt that Lyotard has fully grasped Wittgenstein's perspective on meaning as residing in language use, and he sees clearly enough the importance of Wittgenstein's

Although there is apparently no place for the grammar of a unified self in Lyotard's linguistic scheme of things, there are hints of a recovery of the self in the domain of rhetoric, suggesting a possible postmodern portrait of the self as a rhetorical animal. If Aristotle's book on rhetoric is indeed to be understood as one of the first systematic interpretations of how human beings exist in the world, as Heidegger at one point maintains,[11] then it might behoove us to look into the practical uses of discourse in our discussions of what is good for the polis to see if we might locate the who of discourse as an engaged rhetorical self. Lyotard's interest in rhetoric, however, recalls the ancient Sophists rather than Aristotle. Lyotard's admira-

---

attack on representational theories that construe language as a mirror of essences somehow present in and predicable of things in the world. But in appropriating Wittgenstein's grammar of "language games," he fails to recognize the import of Wittgenstein's notion of the "forms of life" (*Lebensformen*) that provide the background and context against which and in which the language games play out their sense and reference. It is this wider economy of forms of life that supplies the leverage for a life-experiencing discursive subject that is all but obliterated in Lyotard's doctrine of radical heterogeneity.

11. Heidegger was particularly intrigued by Aristotle's discussion of the affects in the second book of his *Rhetoric*. He saw it to be of particular consequence that Aristotle chose to discuss the determinants of mood in his *Rhetoric* rather than in his *De Anima*, and that in doing so Aristotle was able to show that before the affects become discrete data for psychological investigation they display an interpretive understanding of oneself in everyday dealings with other selves. "It is not an accident that the earliest systematic interpretation of affects that has come down to us is not treated in the framework of 'psychology.' Aristotle investigates the πάθη [affects] in the second book of his rhetoric. Contrary to the traditional orientation, according to which *Rhetoric* is conceived as the kind of thing we 'learn in school,' this work of Aristotle must be taken as the first systematic hermeneutic of the everydayness of Being with one another" (*Being and Time*, trans. John Macquarrie and Edward Robinson [New York: Harper and Row, 1962], p. 178).

tion for the Greek Sophists, Protagoras and Gorgias, is indeed quite pronounced, and in a sense Lyotard's version of postmodernism can be understood to involve a reclamation of the rhetoric that the Sophists introduced.[12] But even this appropriation of sophistic rhetoric is subject to a postmodern twist. Making much of the loss of the reality of the referent in sophistical disputation, Lyotard extends the dissolution of reference across both poles—the self-reference of the rhetor and the reality-reference in the object of discourse. Rhetoric sans rhetor and sans referenced reality is subject to the fate of a self-devouring "rhetorical agonistics," a discursive war, waged by the "partisans of agonistics" against the "partisans of dialogue." Needless to say, the status of the "partisans of agonistics" as *partisans* remains undecidable and indeterminate.

Here it is well to proceed with some caution. The claim for an incorrigible heterogeneity of forms of speech and language games may be premature. First, a recognition of diversity, plurality, and multiplicity in the economy of discourse—which, indeed, would seem to be unavoidable—does not warrant claims for heterogeneity. The multiple does not by necessity imply that which is radically "other," as is suggested in the use of *heterogeneous*. The slide from diversity, plurality, and multiplicity to heterogeneity, paralogy, and incommensurability is too hurried, too facile, inviting a skewing of the phenomenon of discourse as it is lived through and more proximately experienced in our quotidian existence. The economy of discourse is more of a

12. Lyotard's interest in the Sophists is centered on their contribution to a "politics of opinion" and its celebration of multiplicity and plurality, countering the demands for unity and totality on the part of the partisans of a "politics of reason" (*Just Gaming*, trans. Wlad Godzich [Minneapolis: University of Minnesota Press, 1985], pp. 82, 95). See also Lyotard's discussion of Protagoras and Gorgias in *The Differend*, pp. 6-19.

mixed discourse than the postmodern separatists are wont to acknowledge.

In its narrational performances the self emplots not only a variety of semiotic forms and rules (phonemic, syntactic, and lexical rules, for example), but also a diversity of semantic tokens and discursive genres. It does so, however, in such a wise that the semiotic and the semantic intermesh and conspire to produce a *mixed* discourse. The speech act "the carburetor malfunctions," uttered by the chief mechanic to his apprentice, is at once a constative and an imperative. It states what is the case and signals to the apprentice that the carburetor is to be fixed. Shakespeare's celebrated line "parting is such sweet sorrow" is at once an aesthetically expressive use of language and an articulation of a truth about human existence. When the moderator at the opening session of the International Congress on World Population remarks that by the year 2050 the population of the world will have doubled, she is at once providing a scientifically based prediction and offering an evaluation and assessment of a developing situation that requires correction. Within the context of our everyday communicative practices there are no walls of separation between the descriptive, normative, prescriptive, imperative, interrogative, and exclamatory functions of discourse. There is rather an inmixing and an overlapping. Nor is the who that is present in each of these functions—the who of description, the who of interrogation, the who of prescription—divided and multiplied, summoning an unmanageable heterogeneity of changing selves.

The recognition of a mixed discourse, extending across the borders of our descriptive, prescriptive, and expressive communicative practices, has a direct bearing not only on a response to the postmodern challenge but also on the legacy of modernity, defined as the "stubborn differentiation" of the culture-spheres of science, morality, and art. Against the backdrop of our explorations into the dynamics of discourse and narrative, it would now appear that the culture-spheres of science, morality, and art cannot be that facilely divided. There is more of an inmixing of the constative or descriptive, the normative or prescriptive, and the expressive or aesthetic across the domains of science, morality, and art than the framers of the modernity problematic are wont to acknowledge. The stories that we tell in our narratival experience exhibit an overlapping and entwinement of scientific, moral, and artistic meanings. Not only in our ordinary discourse in the everyday world do scientific descriptions, moral prescriptions, and artistic expressions slide into one another; such is also the case in the technical discourses that inform expert knowledge in the various scientific and humanistic endeavors. Narratives are told by the vulgar and the learned alike. The long-standing folk wisdom that one should learn to talk with the vulgar while one thinks with the learned needs to be reformulated as an injunction to attend to the inmixing of speech and thought that is operant in both. The narratives of everyday communication and the narratives of expert knowledge alike illustrate a mixed discourse of overlapping interests and joint projects that extend across the boundaries of the science, morality, and art that modernity viewed as stubbornly differentiated.

The overlapping and entwinement of various forms of discourse provides a binding intertextuality that keeps the multiplicity of our language games and the demarcations of the modern culture-spheres from sliding into a radical heterogeneity of events of discourse and an accompanying pluralization of selves that would attach a different who to every different portion of discourse. In our refigured portrait of the self after postmodernity the who of discourse remains present to itself in its multiple forms of speech, diverse language games, and variegated narratives. It is precisely this presence of the who of discourse, illustrating a species of self-identity, that has been found to be so odious by the adherents of postmodernism. So how are we to respond to the postmodern challenge on this specific issue? What is to be said about self-presence and self-identity in the story of the self after postmodernity?

A description (or redescription) of the who of discourse as present to itself as it shifts from one genre of discourse and one language game to another, would do well to begin with an *explicatio via negativa*. The presence of the who is not that of a self-identical monad, mute and self-enclosed, changeless and secured prior to the events of speaking. The presence at issue is localized neither metaphysically in a fixed, underlying substratum nor epistemologically in a prelinguistic, zero-point center of consciousness. The who of discourse is not a "thing," a pre-given entity, a ghost in a machine, or whatever. Nor is the who a pre-given logico-epistemological set of conditions for cognition. The who of discourse is an achievement, an accomplishment, a performance, whose presence to itself is admittedly fragile, subject to forgetfulness and semantic ambiguities. But in all this there is still a unity and a species of self-identity, secured not by an abiding substratum but rather by an achieved self-identity, acquired through a transversal extending over and lying across the multiple forms of speech and language games without coincidence with any one of them. This transversal dynamics, effecting a convergence without coincidence, defines the unity, presence, and identity of the self. And they are a unity, presence, and identity that are concretely manifest in narration, in the telling of the story by the who of discourse, emplotting the multiple and changing episodes of her or his communicative endeavors.

To speak of such an achievement of presence through an emplotment of variable speech acts and language games, to speak of a unification of self amidst diversity—in short, to speak of narrative self-identity—requires clarification of the sense of identity that is at issue. The so-called problem of personal or self-identity has occupied the storm center of many a philosophical controversy. To what extent this problem is a genuine problem and to what extent it is a result of the misalignment of semantic connectors, somewhat akin to what Ryle called a category-mistake, may indeed be worthy of investigation. The bugbear has to do with the sense, or senses, of "sameness" at issue in our grammar of identity. There is what one might call a strong or strict or rigid sense of sameness, illustrated by what is often referred to as the "law of identity," from which we learn that everything is identical with itself. Everything that is, is what it is and not something else. But taken in the strictest sense, this law reduces to a tautology and catapults us into an aporia in which to say that a thing is identical with itself is trivially true and to say that it is identical with something else is patently false. It is thus that the very utility of the grammar of identity becomes questionable, which has prompted some to urge its deletion from the philosophical lexicon as a queer kind of epistemological and metaphysical designator.

Such a straightforward elimination of talk about identity might, however, be premature. Instead, one could play with two senses of identity, differentiated in terms of tendencies and gradations toward a strict sense of identity on the one hand and a more flexible sense on the other hand. Nuances in our everyday discourse attest to the play between these two senses of identity. We speak of things being very much the same, resembling each other to a T. And then we speak of things being more or less the same, quite similar but still different in certain respects. We also speak of something being more or less the same as it has been in the past, indicating that the question of temporality, sameness through time, is at issue in our concerns about identity.

There is thus an evident slackness in our vocabulary of identity—identity can be more or less, very similar or not so similar, close resemblance or partial resemblance. Now, one is able to take up this slack in the interests of conceptual clarification by attending to the gradations moving toward the two poles just referenced—a strict sense of identity versus a more flexible and open-textured sense—and seeing how this might be relevant to our notion of narrative self-identity.

Paul Ricoeur, in his Gifford Lectures *Oneself as Another,* has furrowed a promising path for our present inquiry with his distinction between "*idem*-identity" and "*ipse*-identity." The Latin markers *idem* and *ipse* can be helpful in explaining the more and less strict senses of identity. *Idem*-identity involves an appeal to objective criteria of identification. Finding its touchstone in the oneness of numerical identity, *idem*-identity secures the concept of permanence in time, or more precisely permanence *outside* of time, by analyzing this concept into an unbroken continuity and a rigid immutability. The tradition of Western philosophy found the metaphysical support for such a continuity and immutability in the vocabulary of an abiding substratum that is able to weather the ravages of time and change. *Ipse*-identity, in contrast, is the identity of selfhood, the sense of identity at issue in the occasioning of personal identity, the sense of identity applicable to a person's character, which for Ricoeur finds its direct analogue in "character" as a protagonist in a story.[13]

13. "The person, understood as a character in a story, is not an entity distinct from his or her 'experiences.' Quite the opposite: the person shares the condition of dynamic identity peculiar to the story recounted. The narrative constructs the identity of the character, what can be called his or her narrative identity, in constructing that of the story told. It is the identity of the story that makes the identity of the character" (Paul

Of particular relevance to this distinction between two senses of identity is its applicability to another distinction that emerges in our quotidian conversations, namely, the distinction between persons and things. In introducing the topic of this chapter, the self in discourse, we were at some pains to distinguish a "who" question from a "what" question. Asking the question "Who is speaking?" marks out different parameters of inquiry than does the question "What is the atomic weight of silicon?" Whereas the notion of *idem*-identity has a peculiar applicability to the second question, *ipse*-identity figures decisively in the first. We would become involved in a category-mistake were we to take the one for the other.

Decisive in the distinction between these two kinds of identity is their relation to temporality. *Idem*-identity travels with an external and objectivized concept of time as a serial succession of instants in a determinate order of coming to be and passing away. Entities retain their identity precisely because they remain external to this succession of instants, exhibiting a permanence throughout time, fixed, continuous, and immutable. *Ipse*- or personal identity develops *with* and *in* the temporal becoming of the self, occasioning a presence of the self to itself that is borne by a recollection of that which has been and an anticipation of that which is not yet. The temporality at issue in *ipse*-identity is more like an overlapping of past and future with the present than a serial succession of nows. We shall call this "narrative temporality," linking it directly with an understanding of the self as a storytelling animal. Narrative temporality enables the emplotment of the history of the self as a dynamic coming from a past and moving into a future in such a wise that the past and the future figure as indigenous features of the story

Ricoeur, *Oneself as Another*, trans. Kathleen Blamey [Chicago: University of Chicago Press, 1992], pp. 147–148.

of self as it unfolds. And the identity of self in all this consists in the degree to which the self is able to unify its past accomplishments and its future projects. The self that has nothing to remember and nothing for which to hope is a self whose identity stands in peril.

Because of traditional habits of thought that picture time as a flowing stream, a rapid succession of instants in which things come to be and pass away, it is difficult to find the appropriate grammar to articulate the sense of temporality at issue in narrative identity. It is misleading to speak of the narrating self as being "in" time or existing "throughout" time. The relation between the self and time is of a more intimate sort. The self exists *as temporalized*. Temporality enters into the very constitution of who the self is. Temporality thus need no longer be viewed as an external threat to self-identity, as a coefficient of adversity, as that which ruptures the unity of self by pulverizing it into a flux of changing multiplicities. Narrative temporality enriches rather than impoverishes the self, and the identity of such a temporalized self is not to be mistaken for the abstract and objectivating identity that equates identity with permanence outside of time. The story of the self is a developing story, a story subject to a creative advance, wherein the past is never simply a series of nows that have lapsed into nonbeing, but a text, an inscription of events and experiences, that stands open to new interpretations and new perspectives of meaning. Correspondingly, the future is not a series of nows that has not yet come into being. The future of narrative time is the self as possibility, as the power to be able to provide new readings of the script that has already been inscribed and to mark out new inscriptions of a script in the making.[14]

14. Polkinghorne addresses this point when he writes: "Narrative enrichment occurs when one retrospectively revises, selects, and orders past

In pursuing the question of the who of discourse we are thus led to the profile of a narrative self constituting itself through the inscription of stories within the horizons of a narrative temporality. Michel Foucault used a piquant phrase for the title of his 1983 article *"L'écriture de soi"* ("The Scripting of Self"), which is helpful for articulating what is at issue in our depiction of the self in discourse. Foucault integrates his project of scripting the self with the story of Stoicism, thus making possible a reclamation of insights into the process of self-constitution provided by the Stoics but largely forgotten by the moderns. Canvassing the writings of Seneca and Marcus Aurielius, Foucault sketches a portrait of the Stoic self as a profile in courage, through which the self calls on inner resources to establish an ethos by scripting for itself a style of life wherewith to cope with the misfortunes of nature. The Stoic was bent on stylizing her or his existence, providing it with form and balance, and achieving the maximum harmony in the face of circumstances that remain out of one's control.

Foucault's appeal to the Stoic ethos to flesh out his concept of the scripting of self has its own rewards for advancing a narrational account of self-identity in the odyssey of selfhood. Self-identity does indeed have much to do with ethos, and particularly with ethos as the formation of character. Although there are some indications that Foucault's read on the Stoic ethics tends to blur the distinction between ethics and aesthetics, courting a Nietzschean-like aestheticism in which moral values are aesthetically transvalued, coupling the scripting of

details in such a way as to create a self-narrative that is coherent and satisfying and that will serve as a justification for one's present condition and situation. . . . Identity consists not simply of self-narrative that integrates one's past events into a coherent story, however. It also includes the construction of a future story that continues the 'I' of the person" (*Narrative Knowing and the Human Sciences,* pp. 106–107).

self with the development of character contributes a needed dimension to an account of the narrative self.[15]

It has already been suggested, in concert with reflections on the matter by Paul Ricoeur, that the identity of the narrating self, the self as homo narrans, finds its proper analogue not in an objectivating numerical identity but rather in the self-identity achieved through the development of characters within the plot of a story. The concept of character thus becomes of particular relevance for fleshing out the notion of narrative self-identity. Again taking cues from a Rylean ordinary language perspective, we begin with the quotidian usage of *character* as that which provides the distinctive characteristics or character-marks of a particular individual. Character is that which makes characterization possible, identifying the self in various stages of its developments.

The distinctive characteristics that make up self-identity can profitably be analyzed into the performance of roles, extending further the analogy of personal identity as character, as defined within the scenario of a narration in which plot and characters are integrated. Just as the characters in the narratives of literary invention mark out the roles of the protagonists and the dramatis personae in the epic, the novel, the short story, and the drama, so the characteristics that constitute self-identity in everyday life mark out the roles of speakers and hearers, authors and readers, as they each achieve their respective stances within a panoply of communicative practices.

Although the concept of character as an ensemble of characteristics advances the elucidation of the workings of self-identity, certain pitfalls accompany this usage. Chief among

15. Foucault's move toward a species of aestheticism is documented and discussed further in chapter 2 of this book, "The Self in Action," in connection with an examination of Kierkegaard's doctrine of the three existence-spheres—the aesthetical, the ethical, and the religious.

these is a tendency to analyze character into a solidification of habits and regimentation of roles, buying into the substance-attribute classificatory schema that was used in the traditional doctrine of definition to arrive at a real essence. Within such a scheme of things, character congeals into a collage of attributal properties that inhere in a fixed and timeless substance. That such was the fate of the classical doctrine of definition is well known, and it is precisely the design of the narrational notion of character to avoid this fate. The self-identity of character in the scripting of self retains an open texture, informed by possibilities that the self has not yet actualized, subject to a creative advance toward the future, and as such it should never be construed as simply the sedimentation of past habitual responses.

We are further aided in our effort to elucidate the open texture of self-identity as character formation by consulting the contribution of Julia Kristeva. Both a theorist of linguistics and a practicing psychoanalyst, Kristeva has sketched a portrait of the self against the background of an entwined linguistic and psychoanalytical constitution. What she has chosen to call the "phenomenological subject of enunciation" makes its appearance at the crossroads of semantics and psychological science and emerges from this intersection as a "subject-in-process" (*sujet en procès*) — a dynamic speaking and acting subject in the throes of a creative becoming. In delineating her portrait of the subject of enunciation as a subject-in-process, Kristeva is able to split the difference between the traditional concept of the self as an abiding and immutable substance and the postmodern predilection for an elimination of the vocabularies of subject and subjectivity per se.[16]

16. See particularly Julia Kristeva, *Revolution in Poetic Language,* trans. Margaret Waller (New York: Columbia University Press, 1984), and "The System and the Speaking Subject," in *The Kristeva Reader,* ed. Toril Moi (New York: Columbia University Press, 1986), pp. 24–33.

Of particular relevance to any project of developing a new description of the self is Kristeva's recognition of the need to integrate the speaking subject, the subject of enunciation, with the subject of action. Discourse and the politics of character are seen to slide into one another, coming together in what Kristeva has chosen to call a "politics of marginality." It is a politics leavened by "marginality" because the most effective resources for social change are found in the interventions of marginal groups, after one has become duly suspicious about the grandiose aims of collective political programs. Here we find a clear recognition of the need for some concept of agency, some notion of the self as subject of action.

The process of character formation, through which the self achieves its self-identity in the telling and hearing of stories, requires a thick description so as to incorporate the role of decision and action in the building of character. Although we have borrowed the vocabulary of narrative, plot, and character from the field of literary studies, it is now necessary to extend the significations of this vocabulary into the domains of human action and social practices. As Kristeva reminds us, the subject constitutes itself at the same time as speaking and agentive subject against the backdrop of an ethos and a body politic of common goals and institutional involvements.

Our having landed on narrative as the linchpin in the first profile of our wider portrait of the self thus has some happy consequences for the transition to the second profile, the self in action. Narrative can no longer be considered simply as a determinant of discourse and a format of textuality. Narrative is also an indigenous feature of human action, providing the context and horizon for the emplotment of the multiple activities of the self against the backdrop of a tradition of communicative practices.

2

The Self in Action

The history of both Western and Eastern philosophy has provided numerous and varied accounts of human action. Although it has been only in recent times that philosophy of action has become a specialized subdiscipline, often indexed alongside its sister subdiscipline of philosophy of language, philosophers from early times have had much to say about action, in both its individual and its public display. Not surprisingly, many of these descriptions and analyses of human action were developed in concert with issues relating to ethical behavior and sociopolitical organization.

Our sketch of the profile of the self in discourse, culminating in a notion of narrative self-identity borne by a process of character formation, set the stage for a transition from an exploration of the self in discourse to one of the self in action. This transition, facilitated by a thick description of the meaning of *character,* needs to be made explicit. In doing so it is important to distinguish two senses of narrative, which one might name in a quite pedestrian manner as the weaker and the stronger sense. Narrative in the weaker and more conventional sense is understood as a form and style of discourse and as a literary construct. Narrative in the stronger sense of the term is a form and dynamics of the self as life-experiencing subject. On the one hand we have narrative as a lexical entry for poetics; on the other hand is narrative as expressive of an ontological claim. It is this latter sense of narrative to which David Carr, in his fine book *Time, Narrative, and History,* points when he observes that "narrative form is not a dress which covers something else but the *structure inherent in human experience and action*" (emphasis mine).[1] It is also this sense of narrative that is at issue when Anthony Paul Kerby writes, "Life is inherently of a narrative structure, a structure that we make explicit when we reflect upon our past and our possible future. The actions of human agents, to be intelligible, must be seen against the background of a history, a history of causes and goals, of failure, achievements, and aspirations."[2]

It soon becomes evident that narrative in this stronger sense, understood as an ontological structure of human experience, encompasses the domain of human action. Narrative is not simply the telling of a story by the who of discourse, providing a binding textuality of past and future inscriptions; it is also the emplotment of a personal history through individual and institutional action. Narrative thus provides the proper context for the amalgam of discourse and action that informs and drives the economy of communicative praxis. The concrete spin-off from this broad understanding of narrative for the wider discipline of philosophy is that it installs a complementarity of philosophy of language and philosophy of action, warding off any bifurcation of these two subdisciplines and any tendencies for foundationalist claims on the part of the one or the other. More specifically, a proper emphasis on the relation between discourse and action as an amalgam, sans reduction of the one to the other, provides the needed corrective to certain postmodern predilections toward a pantextualism and linguistification of reality, whereby language and discourse displace the realities of percep-

1. David Carr, *Time, Narrative, and History* (Bloomington: Indiana University Press, 1986), p. 65.
2. Anthony Paul Kerby, *Narrative and the Self* (Bloomington: Indiana University Press, 1991), p. 40.

tion, action, emotions, and the more global experience of self and world.[3]

As we shift our focus of attention from the profile of the self in discourse to the profile of the self in action, it is of some urgency that we attend to the status and role of embodiment. This, of course, is not to say that the body was absent in the preceding discussion of the who of discourse. The speaking and narrating subject announces its presence in full bodily attire. It is in the phenomenon of the self in action, however, that the role of the body moves into prominence, enabling a fleshing out of the portrait of the self after postmodernity in its concrete bodily motility and significance.

It should come as no surprise that a philosophical inquiry into the being and behavior of the human self would need to take up an account of the role of the body in the experience of selfhood. From the dawn of philosophy, in both the Orient and the Occident, philosophers have had much to say about the human body. Plato's celebrated tripartite portrait of the human soul as a composite of reason, spirit, and appetite was sketched against the backdrop of some profound worries about the uneasy alliance of body and soul. In the end, it is the time-bound and vacillating body, according to Plato, that bears the responsibility for deflecting the vision of the mind as it seeks to prehend the world of eternal and immutable forms. The human body thus figures in the thought of Plato as a metaphysical embarrassment, which explains his reference to the body in the *Phaedo* as the "prison house" of the soul.

3. For an extended discussion of how the intertexture of discourse and action informs the dynamics of communicative praxis, avoiding both the reduction of the one to the other and the unacceptable bifurcation of them into separate enclaves, see Calvin O. Schrag, *Communicative Praxis and the Space of Subjectivity* (Bloomington: Indiana University Press, 1986).

A curious thing, however, has happened in the story about the body in Western philosophy as it continued into the twentieth century, and particularly in the account of the role and significance of the body in the philosophy of Michel Foucault. In his book *Discipline and Punish,* Foucault provides a detailed history of the birth and development of the prison as a vehicle for punishment and reform, giving particular attention to the "body of the condemned" as portrayed in the records of the grisly spectacles of torture in the early forms of punishment. Although the modern panoptic principle of surveillance and control, inspired by Jeremy Bentham's architectural symbol of the Panopticon, replaced the severity of the punishment meted out in the early uses of the dungeon and the scaffold, the intent of modernity was not to do away with punishment, or even to punish less, but rather to punish better and with more universality. Now, Foucault finds in this alleged progression from punishment exhibited in dungeons and on the scaffold to punishment exercised through supervision and control an intriguing allegory of the relationship or disrelationship of the human soul with its body. The panoptic prison, with its constant surveillance by ever-present wardens, also tells a story about the human soul and the human body. It tells the story of a prison within the soul itself, admittedly not built of mortar and steel, but nonetheless equipped with a warden who supervises and controls, namely, conscience. Plato simply had it wrong. The soul is the prison of the body![4]

The story of the soul-body relationship from Plato to Foucault, with its somewhat curious inversion concerning which is imprisoned by which, contains a colorful variety of plots be-

4. Michel Foucault, *Discipline and Punish: The Birth of the Prison,* trans. Alan Sheridan (New York: Random House, 1979), p. 30. See also the chapter called "Panopticism," pp. 195–228.

tween the times of ancient Greece and the twilight of the twentieth century. Treatises on the doctrine of the soul, appearing frequently throughout the history of ancient and medieval philosophy, commonly recalled Aristotle's familiar analogy of the soul residing in the body like a pilot residing in his ship.[5] Definitions of the human soul and body proceeded in conjunct with the stock metaphysical schemata of the tradition, including specifically the categories of substance-attribute and form-matter. Interest in the problem continued into the modern period and took on new directions as a result of Descartes's metaphysical dualism, which defined mind and body as distinct and separable substances.

After Descartes it simply became a mark of the philosophical trade to traffic in issues having to do with the "mind-body problem." Every self-respecting philosopher was required to take a position on the problem, either continuing and supporting the Cartesian dualism or devising alternative theories, some with highfalutin-sounding names, such as physicalism, mentalism, epiphenomenalism, interactionism, occasionalism, parallelism, double-aspect theory, doctrine of pre-established harmony, and certain combinations of several of the above. Although one might think that such a proliferation of isms, coupled with rampant theory construction, would bamboozle and deter even the most spirited philosophical souls from further inquiry, this did not happen to be the case. Indeed, well into the twentieth century, disputations by rival theorists on the mind-body problem not only continued but intensified, spawning new theories so as to keep abreast with the most recent developments in cybernetics, artificial intelligence, and cognitive science. There appeared to be no dearth of merchants hawking newly invented

5. Aristotle, *De Anima,* book II, chap. 1, 413a7–9 (*The Basic Works of Aristotle,* ed. Richard McKeon [New York: Random House, 1941], p. 556).

theories on what the human mind is and how it relates to the human body, anticipating the day when these merchants of mind-body theories, like the merchants of the American Express card, would entreat the general populace not to leave home without one.

A curious consequence of the intensified theory construction of the mind-body relation in modern and recent philosophy is the concentrated attention given to the meaning of "mind" and the virtual inattention given to the meaning of "body." The assumption appears to be that everybody in the philosophical neighborhood knows what it means to be a human body, leaving the central task that of getting things straight on the peculiar marks of the mental. The human body, it is presumed, is but an instance of physical bodies in general, existing alongside other bodies that make up the corporeal furniture of the universe, defined through the properties of extension, figure, mass, and motion. Hence, the solution to the problem at issue, it is claimed, requires a theory that is able to explain the correlations and connections between supposed mental states and supposed physical properties.

It is precisely the taken-for-granted concept of the human body as simply a thing among other things, an object among other objects, an extension of material substance in general, that needs to be problematized. An inquiry into the meaning of embodiment, as it pertains to the self as the who of discourse and the who of action, requires that one move beyond the traditional metaphysical prejudgments of the human body as an entity defined within the coordinates of extension, mass, and motion, congealed and solidified as an *ob-ject*, somehow standing over against the mind that putatively perceives it. In pursuing the question "What does it mean to exist *as embodied?*" which is unavoidable if one is to come to grips with the phenomenon of self-knowledge, one would advance the cause by declaring a moratorium on the accelerated production of theories about the mind-body relation, in which both "mind" and "body" are objectified abstractions, and focusing instead on the praxis-oriented understanding of the self in its concrete bodily involvements and activities.

Fortunately, in our task of mounting an inquiry into the human self as embodied we do not need to start at point zero because there is already a sizable literature on the topic of embodiment. Much of this literature has been inspired by Maurice Merleau-Ponty's seminal descriptions and analyses of the structure and dynamics of what he came to call "the lived body" (*le corps vécu*), which he distinguished from the human body as an object for a physiological mechanics that derived its categorial matrix and principles of explanation from investigations of material substance in general.[6] But Merleau-Ponty was not alone in coming upon the philosophical consequence of distinguishing the human body as lived in our everyday involvements and practices from the human body as an object for scientific and metaphysical explanation. Gabriel Marcel, prior to Merleau-Ponty's more systematic phenomenology of the lived body, had already pointed to the phenomenon at issue in his concrete existential reflections on embodiment, which he later summed up rather nicely in his Gifford Lectures, *The Mystery of Being,* delivered at the University of Aberdeen in 1949 and 1950: "My body is *my* body just in so far as I do *not* consider it in this detached fashion, do not put a gap between myself and it. To put

6. See particularly Maurice Merleau-Ponty, *The Phenomenology of Perception,* trans. Colin Smith (New York: Humanities Press, 1962), and especially "Part One: The Body," pp. 67–199. For an elegant explication of the principal topics in the philosophy of Merleau-Ponty see M. C. Dillon, *Merleau-Ponty's Ontology* (Bloomington: Indiana University Press, 1988). Chapter 8 of Dillon's book, "The Lived Body," pertains directly to the issue at stake in the concept of embodied action.

this point in another way, my body is mine in so far as for me my body is not an object, but rather, I *am* my body."[7]

Jean-Paul Sartre, the compatriot and kindred philosophical spirit of both Marcel and Merleau-Ponty on this issue, supplemented the literature on embodiment during his time by focusing on the linkage of embodiment and human action against the backdrop of his existential philosophy of human involvement (*engagement*), which centered on the "human situation" as at once the point of departure for philosophical reflection and the region of its return. Sartre succeeds in consolidating his perspective on embodiment in a typical Sartrian one-liner when he writes that "the body . . . appears within the limits of the situation as a synthetic totality of *life* and *action*."[8] Interest in the phenomenon of embodiment, however, was not confined to mid-twentieth-century French philosophers, writing from the then-popular perspectives of existentialism and phenomenology. On the North American continent this interest was expressed by William James, quite in advance of the philosophical breakthroughs in Europe at mid-century. In his *Essays in Radical Empiricism*, first published in 1912, James anticipates the preoccupations with the theme of embodiment that followed some decades later: "The world experienced (otherwise called the 'field of consciousness') comes at all times with our body as its centre, centre of vision, centre of action, centre of interest."[9]

In more recent times, Bruce Wilshire has provided an elu-

7. Gabriel Marcel, *The Mystery of Being,* vol. 1, trans. G. S. Fraser (Chicago: Henry Regnery, 1960), p. 123. For a discussion on embodiment as it relates to the distinction between "being" and "having" see his earlier work *Etre et avoir* (Fernand Aubier: Editions Montaigne, 1935).

8. Jean-Paul Sartre, *Being and Nothingness: An Essay in Phenomenological Ontology,* trans. Hazel Barnes (New York: Philosophical Library, 1956), p. 346.

9. William James, *Essays in Radical Empiricism* (New York: Longmans, Green, 1942), p. 170n.

cidation of embodiment in connection with the phenomenon of "enactment" as illustrated in the metaphorics of the theater. The underlying argument in Wilshire's provocative work that addresses the relation of embodiment and enactment, *Role Playing and Identity: The Limits of Theatre as Metaphor,* is that metaphors of the theater, such as enactment of roles, mimetic responses, and body-images, inform the drama of everyday life. In this illustration of artistic metaphors, wherewith theater provides us with lenses the better with which to see ourselves, the phenomenon of embodiment plays a pivotal role. The enactment of roles, whether on stage or off, involves an intercalation of mimesis and embodiment, each reinforcing the other in the achievement of self-identity. "To be a self is to be a human body that is mimetically involved with other such bodies, but that nevertheless has a capacity to distinguish itself consciously from others and to regard its history and its prospects as its own."[10] In using the metaphorics of theater, with regard to both its applications and its limitations for a comprehension of the narrativity of everyday life, Wilshire is able to couple embodiment and enactment in such a manner that they illustrate the joint achievement of bodily and narrative self-identity.

The efforts of Gilbert Ryle for effecting a much needed deconstruction of the official Cartesian doctrine of mind as a mental substance have already been applauded in the previous chapter. Descartes construed the mind as an entity housed in a body subject to mechanical laws—a ghostly Robinson Crusoe residing in a machine, was Ryle's way of putting the matter.[11] The task that Ryle bequeathed to his successors is that of continuing and expanding his original project by effecting a cor-

10. Bruce Wilshire, *Role Playing and Identity: The Limits of Theatre as Metaphor* (Bloomington: Indiana University Press, 1982), p. 266.
11. Gilbert Ryle, *The Concept of Mind* (New York: Barnes and Noble, 1949), p. 13.

responding deconstruction of the official Cartesian doctrine of the human body as a queer kind of soft machine. The doctrine of the self as a ghost in a machine needs to be attacked from both sides, as it were—from the side of mind preconceived as an apparition of mental properties and from the side of the body preconceived as a mechanistic composite of external parts.

Deconstructing the concept of the human body as a machine, as a physiological mechanism, involves the difficult task of devising a vocabulary to articulate the perception, the experience, and the understanding of our bodies as they figure in our everyday preoccupations and practices. Indeed, speaking of "our bodies," "my body," or "having a body" may already be problematic, prejudging the body as a possession, something that one owns, like a wardrobe of garments. Within such a perspective the body becomes externalized, a thing among other things, which somehow in this case just happens to belong to me. But our everyday practices, habits, and skills testify to a more intimate connection of mind with body. Also, the very grammar of "being in" tends to obscure the phenomenon of body as experienced, as for example in speaking of the self being "in" its body as a pilot is "in" his ship. Because of these possible misdirections in the vocabulary pertaining to the human body, some philosophers, and particularly those working from a phenomenology of embodiment, prefer the locutions "lived body," "embodied existence," "incarnate consciousness," and "I *am* my body" (as opposed to "I *have* a body"), as providing a corrective to the externalization and objectivization of the body as a thing among things, a disposable possession that the self might or might not own.

The shift in vocabulary from "having a body" to "being embodied" and "existing-as-embodied" has been designed to problematize the concept of the human body as some species of external garment that the self somehow possesses, clearing the path to an understanding of the body in its lived concreteness as the body-as-myself. Such an understanding of the body opens another perspective on the issue of self-identity that we addressed in chapter 1 in our discussion of narrative identity. We made much of the distinction between narrative identity as descriptive of the phenomenon of selfhood and the objectivating concept of identity as a designator of the immutable sameness of inert objects and things. We are now in a position to see how our previously articulated narrative self-identity is reinforced by a complementing bodily self-identity.

To bring the notion of the self-identity of embodiment into sharper relief, it may be helpful to review briefly the role of the body in classical and modern concepts of individuation and personal identity. The ancient and medieval approaches to the issue proceeded against the backdrop of a bold application of the metaphysical categories of substance-attribute and form-matter. Recognizing the need for something that individuates particulars that possess the same form, the ancients and the medievals were motivated to appeal to the human body as the source of individuation. Human beings are similar by virtue of possessing the form of *animal rationale;* they are different because they have different bodies. It is thus the body that functions as the principle of individuation. It does so, however, not in its lived concreteness but somewhat curiously as an abstract *materia signata quantitate.* This "signate matter," although amorphous, is not wholly indeterminate. It possesses a propensity to take on form, signifying in each particular individual a resident form of humanity. Within such a conceptual scheme, in which the human self is defined as a mixture of formal determinants and material propensities, the occasioning of individuation and personal identity is fated to remain wrapped in impenetrable mists.

The explanatory devices invented by modernity to give an

account of self-identity did not fare much better than did the metaphysics of form and matter in the classical period. In its turn to the subject, modernity searched for a principle of self-identity in an interiorized consciousness, which in becoming conscious of itself as conscious would then latch on to a monadic sameness that remained immune to the rancor of temporal becoming. But the identity that was sought was the *idem*-identity of a changeless substratum exhibiting the criterion of rigid immutability, an identity that eludes all determinations of reference in the personal and social history of the human self. Ironically, this construal of identity as the defining mark of the modern concept of consciousness was destined to remain outside the range of modernity's postulated epistemic signifiers, as David Hume in particular was able to demonstrate almost effortlessly.

The identity at work in the modern concept of the human body, which was placed at a distance from consciousness, also remained elusive—and indeed more so. Undergoing constant change, sometimes greater and sometimes less, destined for a dismemberment of its parts, the human body would remain a most unlikely candidate for identity in the modern scheme of things. Pictured as a composition of parts external to each other, functioning according to the rules of mechanics, which modernity was disposed to equate with the rules of external nature, the body exemplified at most a contingent unity, providing a decidedly unstable receptacle for consciousness. Ryle's characterization of the Cartesian legacy in the modern concept of mind as a ghost in a machine is thus peculiarly apt. The Cartesian invention of mind as a ghostly interior travels with the Cartesian invention of the human body as a mechanism of interlocking parts. Mind and body alike, in the modern view, are abstracted from the incarnate consciousness of the self as embodied.

In the wake of the dismantling of the modern invention of the human body as a soft machine, as a contingent arrangement of external parts conjoined with an interiorized and enigmatic ghost that somehow resides in it, we are able to move to another terrain. This is the terrain on which one encounters the body as lived—a terrain on which the who as an amalgam of discourse and action is called into being as an *embodied who*. And it is in this embodiment that the self-identity of the who achieves another decisive expression, as it already had achieved such an expression in its emplotment as a narrative self-identity. The body as lived is not an external indicator of an "I" or a "me" residing somewhere within it. The body as lived is veritably *who I am*. We can say with Marcel "I am my body," and by this we mean that the self-identity that one articulates in one's storytelling is always entwined with a self-identity of bodily intentionality and motility. In giving an account of the tiredness of my body, I am relating to my hearers that *I am tired*. The story of my body shaking with fear is a story of *my being afraid*. In saying that my nerves are frazzled I am announcing that *I am nervous*. My body as lived is who I am. This is not to be construed as a reduction of mind to matter in the classical or modern sense of reductionism. It is not that we are reducing one entity (mind) to another entity (body), for the who of embodiment is not an entity at all—at least not on the level of a praxis-oriented understanding of self and world. The who of bodily intentionality and motility is older than the entitative abstractions that have been such a bane for theoretical construction as it relates to the mind-body problem.

Having furrowed a path around the classical and modern concepts of mind and body as objectifiable entities within an epistemological framework of knowledge as representation, and having found that the presence of such putatively re-presentable entities is perpetually deferred, we are in a position to offer new descriptions of the embodied self as locus and center of action. The body as concrete embodiment is the site of tasks to be performed and projects to be carried through. The body as lived is that from which something is done. It is the "here" of one's projects. It is the space in which and from which activities are launched and undertaken. But the here and the space at issue, from which action originates, are not the here of an abstracted geometrical point and the space of an abstracted extensive continuum. The space of the body, or more precisely *embodied spatiality*, is not a serialized juxtaposition of points, constituting a vacuum or void that a variety of things at different times happen to occupy. Indeed, the body as a dimension of selfhood does not *occupy* space—at least not in the sense that one would speak of a coffee cup taking up room in its being placed on the table, or being placed anywhere for that matter. The body *inhabits* space; it does not simply *occupy* it. The space at issue in our narrative of the human body is what Merleau-Ponty has variously and suggestively named "lived space," "oriented space," and the "spatiality of situation" as contrasted with the quantitatively measured "spatiality of position."[12]

Correspondingly, the movement displayed in this embodied spatiality as the source and dynamics of action is itself a concrete movement, a movement of engagement, a movement that reaches out to the world in the manipulation of tools and utensils, in the handling and perception of objects, and in the acknowledgement of the presence of other selves through various gestural comportments—the handshake, the caress, the kiss, the laugh, the cry, the intimidating stare. The movement of embodiment must not be confused with a calculus of motion that measures the traversing of objects across adjacent points. The movement of the body as motility, motivation, and dy-

12. *The Phenomenology of Perception*, p. 100.

namics of action is a manifestation of forces and power oriented toward self-actualization and societal interaction. On this particular point Gilles Deleuze's notion of the self as an assemblage of forces and Michel Foucault's accentuation of bio-power in self-formation offer some helpful insights. Indeed, a singular contribution of the postmodern literature has been to call the world's attention to the role of power and the play of active and reactive forces across the spectrum of individual and social practices and scientific and political institutions.

Deleuze's portrait of the rhizomatic self, energized by a play of active and reactive forces, shaped by the contours of a politics of desire, is particularly germane to my own project of devising a sketch of the human subject. Although profoundly suspicious of "subjectivity" as a philosophically useful category, principally because of its close association with interiority, Deleuze has nonetheless tracked a dynamics of subject-formation that effects a passage between the Scylla of an enervating static constitution and the Charybdis of a formless and chaotic indeterminacy. Deleuze's take on the formation of the subject, as Constantin Boundas has documented, develops against the backdrop of his notion of the *chaosmos,* the world as a *becoming-*world, in which the constituted subject emerges not as a "substantive *hypokeimenon*" but rather as a task and a performance in the "theater of philosophy."[13]

There is, however, a problematic tendency, in both Deleuze's politics of desire and Foucault's ontology of power, that requires a corrective. This is the tendency to valorize and celebrate the dynamics of desire and the effects of power at the expense of the role of rationality in the life of the self-constituting sub-

13. See Constantin V. Boundas, "Deleuze: Serialization and Subject-Formation," in *Gilles Deleuze and the Theatre of Philosophy,* ed. C. V. Boundas and D. Olkowski (New York: Routledge, 1994), pp. 99–116.

ject. The self as concretely embodied motility, exhibiting lines of active and reactive forces and displaying the power to initiate action, exercises a peculiar claim on praxis-oriented reason. In such gestural comportment as caressing the arm of a beloved and in such skilled performance as swimming the length of the stadium we observe a bodily comprehension of the world, a dynamics of discernment, an economy of practical wisdom that exhibits its own insight without needing to wait on the determinations of pure cognition and pure theory.

The lived body displays its attunement to an everyday world of practical and personal concerns by grasping and pointing. In the grasping of the pen for writing a letter to a friend, the surrounding lived space is organized in a particular way. Pointing expands the range of the body's inhabiting the world by incorporating social significations. One grasps for oneself in the presence of the other. One points for the other in the presence of oneself. In the concrete motility of grasping and pointing, gesturing and posturing, a praxis-oriented discernment and understanding of self and world is called into being. Postmodernists for the most part have been too quick to dismiss some of the more durable contributions of phenomenology, and in particular the phenomenological notion of "functioning intentionality." To be sure, many of the postmodern critiques of classical phenomenology are on target, and this includes the postmodern assault on "act intentionality" as a transcendental structure of consciousness. But objectivating and constituting act intentionality should never be mistaken for the concretely functioning intentionality that is operative in embodied communicative practices.

The who of action, comprehending the world in and through his or her action, is thus an embodied subject with idiosyncratic features of lived spatiality and lived motility. This distinguishes the self as body from bodies in external and objectivized space, the movements of which are explained by the laws of mechanics. It is this latter notion of body, the Cartesian *res extensa*, that we have sought to deconstruct, showing its inapplicability to the concretely lived body of the human subject.

The human body is not a thing, not an object, not an entity somehow representative of finite substance in general. Indeed, it is the human body, the body as lived, that first provides the conditions for objectification. The human body, although not an object, is that which makes it possible for there to be objects. It is by virtue of my embodiment that the perceived vase on the table becomes *ob-ject*, "stands-over-against," assumes the status of *Gegenstand*. The malfunctioning lawn mower intrudes on my project of mowing the lawn by becoming an objectified entity, a piece of equipment that has lost its serviceability and stands in the way of completing the project at hand. Now, the peculiarities of the situation of embodiment are such that it also provides the conditions for self-objectification—conditions that, it should be emphasized, are not as such conditions for self-alienation. We need to avoid collapsing all forms of objectification into alienation. The embodied self can indeed become an object to itself. It can study itself "objectively"—as it does in the disciplines of physiology, anatomy, microbiology, and psychology. Such scientific studies of the human body clearly retain their intrinsic merit. The problem that occasioned our requirement for a deconstruction of the official Cartesian doctrine of the body as a soft machine, supplementing Professor Ryle's deconstruction of the official Cartesian doctrine of the mind as a ghost in a machine, was not the use of objectifying procedures in scientific inquiry but rather an objectivization of the body on the level of ontological construction, inviting a reductionism of the motility of the human body to an instance of mechanistically determined particles in motion.

Having secured the body as the center of vision and the cen-

ter of action, we are now able to move on to some centrifu-
gal features involving the dialectic of acting and suffering as
the appropriate backdrop for the self-implicature of the who of
action as at once agent and patient. The grammar of dialectics is particularly suitable for a description of the topography
of action because it highlights the dynamism in the coupling
of forces that issue from the economy of embodied engage-
ments, skills, and performances — an active or originating force
and a reactive or responding force. The dynamic of human
action occurs within the span of tension between these two
poles. There is the moment of the inauguration of action, con-
summating the decision to do *x* or *y*, but this moment of inauguration is never an unconditioned or absolute beginning. It
is always in some manner a response to prior action. The who
of action, implicated in the experience of making a decision,
is thus at once agent and patient, an initiator of action and a
receiver of action, doing the acting while responding to prior
action.

From this dialectic of acting and suffering we derive a twofold truth, namely, that the human self called into being as
a coupling of discourse and action is neither a sovereign and
autonomous self, whose self-constitution remains impervious
to any and all forces of alterity, nor a self caught within the
constraints of heteronomy, determined by forces acting upon
it. The self as the who of action lives *between* autonomy and
heteronomy, active and reactive force, pure activity and pure
passivity. The grammatical voice of action is the middle voice,
neither a sovereign active voice nor a subordinated passive
voice. Suzanne Kemmer, in her carefully researched volume *The
Middle Voice*, provides an illuminating discussion of the middle
voice as a semantic category that is not the property of a specific language, like Greek for example, but is rather orthogonal
to a variety of languages extending across cultural genres and

historical epochs.[14] Deleuze has found an analogous exemplification of the middle voice in his explication of the play of forces in the dynamics of self-becoming. The dichotomy of the active and the passive is for Deleuze a bogus dichotomy, which needs to be dismantled to make visible the dynamic functioning of the infinitive. It is in the play of the infinitive that active and passive forces interact in such a manner as to yield a mutual interdependence.[15] Such an existence "between" the poles of activity and passivity, comprising the self as a dialectic of initiating and receiving action, is a defining feature of the finitude that is characteristic of the self as mortal.

This limitation within the very structure of human finitude does not, however, diminish the importance and urgency of choice in the odyssey of self-constitution and self-understanding. The who of action exercises a genuine freedom as she or he is implicated as a seat and source of empowerment within the wider economy of prior and contemporary co-actors. And here one is able to take a line from Ricoeur's phenomenology of the will, reinforcing the notion of a hermeneutical self-implicature through action. Ricoeur tracks the self-recognition of the agentive subject by exploring what he calls the phenomenon of a "prereflexive imputation of myself" in the act of deciding. An imputation of self is at work in the throes of decision making. "*Je me décide,*" reads the French. "*Ich entscheide*

14. Suzanne Kemmer, *The Middle Voice* (Philadelphia: John Benjamins, 1993).

15. Constantin Boundas succeeds in consolidating this central point in Deleuze's doctrine of subject-formation when he writes, "Forces seized in actu, liberated from substances that function as their support and vehicle, do seem better candidates for a diagrammatic mapping out of becoming: infinitives name forces that are neither active nor passive but both at once, since the quasi-causal function of the infinitive is always already reversible" (*Gilles Deleuze and the Theatre of Philosophy*, p. 105).

mich," reads the German. In English, and probably somewhat cumbersomely, it falls out as "I make up my mind in the act of deciding." At any event, at issue in this multilingual exposé is the recognition that in the dynamics of decision making the who of action is called into being as an agentive subject.[16]

Thus, although the subject implicated in and called into being by its deliberation, decision, and action is not a sovereign and autonomous subject, secure in an abiding and monadic self-identity, it is a genuine agent of change in its consensual and dissensual responses to prior action upon it. The who of action can make a difference in the world of communicative praxis. The who is implicated as the source of empowerment and the agency of enactment. Although neither a metaphysical substrate nor an epistemological zero-point origin, the self as an implicate of action exhibits the power to become an effective agent of social change and cultural transformation. Such is the portrait of the self after postmodernity, after the realization that the postmodern announcement of the death of the subject, like the news release of the death of Mark Twain, was a bit of an exaggeration. One of the recurring ironies of postmodernity, both as a philosophical persuasion and a cultural milieu, is the impassioned call for empowerment alongside requiems eulogizing the passing of the subject as speaker, author, actor—and pretty much in every sense conceivable. But one then needs to ask, "Empowerment by and for whom?" As the anti-Hegelians— Feuerbach, Marx, and Kierkegaard—made us aware of the profound irony of a system of thought without a concrete thinker, so a response to the postmodern challenge requires that we call attention to the analogous irony of discourse without speakers, texts without authors, and action without actors.

16. Paul Ricoeur, *Freedom and Nature: The Voluntary and the Involuntary,* trans. Erazim Kohak (Evanston: Northwestern University Press, 1966), p. 58.

The situating of speakers, authors, and actors within an intentionality of embodiment functioning at the interstices of activity and passivity, doing and suffering, vitalizes and enriches the self as a source of empowerment. This recognition of a dynamics of bio-power in the life of the self announces a more robust sense of self-identity as one observes the slide of narrative self-identity into the domain of embodied action. The self-identity achieved through the emplotment of the who of discourse blends with the bodily self-identity achieved through the enactments of the who of action. It is in this wider perspective that self-identity appears in the guise of *self-constancy* and *existential continuity*.

The most illuminating account in the literature of the self-identity of the who of action, borne by self-constancy and existential continuity, has been provided by Søren Kierkegaard in his epoch-making *Either/Or: A Fragment of Life*. In Kierkegaard's narrative of the self, it is the act of choosing that centralizes the self and occasions its unity and continuity, however fragile this unity and continuity might be, given the factors of human finitude. Addressing the young aesthete, Kierkegaard's protagonist, Judge William, makes matters quite clear with regard to the conditions for the achievement of selfhood. And these conditions have to do not so much with the particulars that happen to be chosen, but with the "reality of the act of choice," and it is through the act of choice that the self constitutes itself. "Even the richest personality," says Judge William, "is nothing before he has chosen himself, and on the other hand even what one might call the poorest personality is everything when he has chosen himself."[17] It is this accentuation of choice that provides the peculiar hallmark of Kierkegaard's existen-

17. Søren Kierkegaard, *Either/Or: A Fragment of Life*, vol. 2, trans. David F. Swenson and Lillian M. Swenson (Princeton: Princeton University Press, 1949), p. 150.

tial reflections on the experience of self. And it is precisely by placing the accent on choosing that Kierkegaard is able to effect his own deconstruction of the official Cartesian "I think, therefore I am." The abstract intellectualism of the Cartesian principle of all principles is dismantled on the way to its refiguration into "I choose, therefore I am."

The connection between choice and self-identity, which we are to understand as intrinsic rather than extrinsic, is the centerpiece of Kierkegaard's account in *Either/Or*. Self-identity is an achievement that is won through the hard struggle of making choices. Hence, Judge William speaks of the soul being "matured in the hour of decision" and of the requirement to choose in such a manner as to achieve an existential continuity. "So the individual chooses himself as a concretion determined in manifold ways, and he chooses himself therefore in accord with his continuity."[18] It is this recurring emphasis on continuity and

18. *Either/Or*, pp. 133, 211. The redescription of self-identity as a self-constancy achieved in response to the demands for deliberation and decision is also a notable feature of Heidegger's analysis of the care-structure of *Dasein* in his monumental work *Being and Time*—a work that would appear to be more indebted to the thought of Kierkegaard than the author either realized or was prepared to acknowledge. Heidegger makes the theme of self-constancy a centerpiece in his explication of authenticity as steadfastness and resoluteness (*Entschlossenheit*). "In terms of care the *constancy of the Self*, as the supposed persistence of the *subjectum*, gets clarified. But the phenomenon of this authentic potentiality-for-Being also opens our eyes for the *constancy of the Self* in the sense of its having achieved some sort of position. The *constancy of the Self*, in the double sense of steadiness and steadfastness, is the *authentic* counter-possibility to the non-Self-constancy which is characteristic of irresolute falling. Existentially, '*Self-constancy*' signifies nothing other than anticipatory resoluteness. The ontological structure of such resoluteness reveals the existentiality of the Self's Selfhood" (Martin Heidegger, *Being and Time*, trans. John Macquarrie and Edward Robinson [New York: Harper and Row], p. 369).

constancy that marks the pivotal and distinguishing feature of Kierkegaard's notion of self-identity—a self-identity informed by choice, decision, and action. We immediately recognize this self-identity to be of the same stripe as that which has been elaborated in the preceding chapter in addressing the topic of the self in discourse. What is at issue is not the strict or rigid sense of identity—identity as an objective criteria for identification, transhistorical and transtemporal, applicable in the realm of abstracted relations of number and quantity. Instead, at issue is the texture of identity descriptive of a *narrative self-identity*, illustrated in the life of the temporalized who of discourse, integrating the past, present, and future into a coherent story.

Having proceeded to an examination of the self in action, we are now able to see how the more fluid and flexible *ipse*-identity, as defined by Ricoeur, applies to the self-identity that is at issue in the existential continuity and constancy of the deciding and acting self. The self in action is a unified self to the extent that it displays a constancy in its discourse and action, in the keeping of its word and in the coherence of its actions, in the delivering of its past promises and in its pre-enactment of commitments for the future. It is thus that conjugal love becomes for Judge William a telling exemplar of self-constancy and existential continuity. This stands in contrast to the romantic love of the young aesthete who experiments with love but never commits himself in marriage, whose past consists of successive experimental relationships that have now gone by and are simply forgotten, whose future is a rarified field of possibilities that may become actual someday, and whose present is defined as a perpetual escape from commitment and responsibility. The fractured and fragmented life of the aesthete is dispersed and discontinuous because he is able to find himself neither in his past nor in his future, as he flees from the responsibility of decision in the present. Such a self, like the "unhappy consciousness" portrayed in Hegel's *Phenomenology* (after which Kierkegaard's portrait of the aesthete would appear to be patterned at least in part), is unable to achieve self-presence because it is neither present to itself in recollection nor present to itself in anticipation.

This fragmentation of the self at the heart of its temporal being, severing the self as past from the self as future, destines the self to a life of despair. It is this that provides the centralizing motif in Kierkegaard's classic phenomenology of despair, *The Sickness unto Death.* The "sickness unto death" at stake in Kierkegaard's slim but profoundly penetrating treatise is precisely despair. Clearly, what we are dealing with here is not death as biological cessation, the death of the deathbed, but rather a *living* death in which the self experiences an alienation from its past and from its future. And without past and future there can be no meaningful, life-affirming present.

The principal lesson to be learned from Kierkegaard's account of the achievement of self-identity through self-constancy has to do with the role of choice and decision in the journeying of the self as a who of action. It is by dint of self-constancy that an integrity of selfhood, as an integration of past and future into the folds of the present, is achieved. However, Kierkegaard has no illusions about the ineradicable contingency and fragility that accompanies the adventure of selfhood. Given the threats of self-alienation, and particularly as manifested in the phenomenon of despair, self-identity remains frail and fractured, subject to the multiple adversities that all human flesh is heir to.

Of additional importance in Kierkegaard's descriptions of self-constancy as it is achieved throughout a life of commitment is the highlighting of the bonding of self with other selves. The integrity that is won through self-constancy is sustained not only through a proper relation of the self to itself but also in and through the self's relation to other selves. In marking out the terrain over which the self travels, Kierkegaard makes it explicit that "this self which is the aim is not merely a personal self but a social, a civic self."[19] It is thus necessary to keep in mind the wider context of Kierkegaard's elucidation of the self as presented in his doctrine of the three "stages of existence" — or "existence-spheres," as they might more appropriately be named — of the aesthetical, the ethical, and the religious.

Kierkegaard's doctrine of the existence-spheres is reminiscent of the much discussed culture-spheres of modernity that are receiving such widespread attention in the current literature. Indeed, the threefold delineation of the aesthetical, the ethical, and the religious comprises Kierkegaard's own overture toward an articulation of the modernity-problem, an overture in which the alleged problem is reframed and refigured. In the process of this refiguration religion is granted a more independent role than is allowed for in the Weberian and Habermasian construal of modernity as involving exclusively the spheres of science, morality, and art. Also, Kierkegaard's doctrine involves a different explication of the way the spheres are first distinguished and then related.

The journey of selfhood, for Kierkegaard, is a journey through the three existence-spheres in such a manner that they can be seen as dialectically constitutive of what is means to be a self. Surely Kierkegaard is misread if the three spheres are construed as successive stages of development in the process of which the earlier stage is left behind in the advance of the later. Admittedly, it is the transition to the ethical stage that heralds the achievement of existential self-identity through a baptism of the will in the act of choosing. Judge William remains quite clear about that: "The act of choosing is essentially a proper

19. *Either/Or*, p. 220.

and stringent expression of the ethical." Yet, with equal emphasis, Kierkegaard's protagonist makes it clear that after the choice "the whole of the aesthetical comes back again in its relativity."[20] The principal point here is that in the process of self-formation the aesthetical is refigured rather than repudiated. It remains a dimension of selfhood, but it becomes relativized, incorporated as a moment in the dialectic of the self-experience. It is no longer the absolute, the alpha and the omega, the sole and all-absorbing preoccupation, as is the case in the life of the young aesthete, Kierkegaard's existential exemplification of Mozart's Don Giovanni.

The issue concerning the relation of the aesthetical to the ethical after the moment of choice requires more attention than can be given to it in the present project. It is clear, however, that Kierkegaard was intent on securing a significant role for the aesthetical while combating any and all tendencies toward an aestheticism in which aesthetics would provide the ultimate measure and aim for self and societal development. The relation of the aesthetical to the ethical also takes on considerable importance in dealing with the challenge of the postmodern ethos, in which tendencies toward a global aestheticism emerge from time to time. A case in point is the thought of Michel Foucault, whose contribution toward filling the void that ensued from the deconstruction of the subject as a metaphysical presence or a vacuous transcendental condition surely needs to be recognized. He made it quite clear, particularly in his later works, that his principal concerns all along were with the being and behavior of the human subject. He saw his genealogical project as geared toward a restoration of a viable sense of subjectivity, a project of restoration that reached a dramatic denouement in his sketch of an "ethic of care for the self as a practice of freedom." Re-

20. *Either/Or*, pp. 141, 150.

sponding to his interviewer's questions about a possible shift in his reflections on ethics and human freedom, moving away from earlier preoccupations with discourse analysis and power relations to a focus on the "hermeneutics of the subject" in which the problem of subjectivity and truth becomes central, Foucault replied, "In fact, that has always been my problem, even if I have expressed in different terms the framework of this thought. I have tried to discover how the human subject entered into games of truth, whether they be games of truth which take on the form of science or which refer to a scientific model, or games of truth like those that can be found in institutions or practices of control."[21]

Yet it remains problematic whether Foucault has been successful in reconstituting the subject within the space of an ethic of care without having the project congeal into a program of *aesthetic* self-formation. Although in his later writings he pays homage to the Stoics for recommending a scripting of self informed by a courage to meet life's challenges, his appreciation of Stoicism is clearly colored by a fascination for the aesthetical. This became abundantly explicit in one of his later interviews in which he related what he had learned from the Stoics: "I don't think one can find any normalization, in, for instance, the Stoic ethics. The reason is, I think, that the principal aim, the principal target of this kind of ethics was an aesthetic one.

21. *The Final Foucault*, ed. James Bernauer and David Rasmussen (Cambridge: MIT Press, 1988), p. 1. See also Foucault's essay "The Subject and Power" in *Michael Foucault: Beyond Structuralism and Hermeneutics*, ed. Hubert L. Dreyfus and Paul Rabinow (Chicago: University of Chicago Press, 1982): "I would like to say, first of all, what has been the goal of my work during the last twenty years. It has not been to analyze the phenomenon of power, nor to elaborate the foundations of such an analysis. . . . it is not power, but the subject, which is the general theme of my research" (p. 208).

First, this kind of ethics was only a problem of personal choice. Second, it was reserved for a few people in the population; it was not a question of giving a pattern of behavior for everybody. It was a personal choice for a small elite. The reason for making this choice was the *will* to live a beautiful life."[22]

This begins to sound very much like what Kierkegaard would call the absolutization of the aesthetical existence-sphere. It also recalls Nietzsche's proclamations that we have art so as not to die of truth and that "it is only as an *aesthetic phenomenon* that existence and the world are eternally *justified.*"[23] Foucault's high regard for Nietzsche is well documented. And as Nietzsche's transvaluation of all hitherto existing values courted a collapse of ethics into aesthetics, morality into art, so Foucault's scripting or rescripting of the self appears to encounter similar problems. This may indeed be a problem endemic to postmodern thought itself, from Nietzsche to the present. In valorizing the economy of the aesthetical, placing a premium on matters of style, postmodernists have responded to the separation of the culture-spheres in modernity by according a ubiquity to the aesthetical. This explains, in part, their readiness to privilege the third of Kant's three *Critiques,* countering the claim of the Marburg School of Kant-interpretation that gave primacy to the first *Critique* as well as the interpretation of the Heidelberg School, which attributed primacy to the second *Critique.* In their efforts to find the cultural apogee in aesthetics rather than in either science or morality, postmodernists have effected a recovery and renewed interest in Nietzsche. Such interest may indeed be well and good, for there is much to learn from Nietz-

22. Quoted in James Miller, *The Passion of Michel Foucault* (New York: Simon and Schuster, 1993), p. 346.

23. Friedrich Nietzsche, *The Birth of Tragedy*, trans. Walter Kaufmann (New York: Vintage Books, 1967), p. 52.

sche, and certainly Nietzsche has been unduly marginalized in many philosophical circles. But there is a growing consensus that an equally passionate recovery and renewal of interest in the thought of Kierkegaard is a requirement of the times. Such a recovery would contribute greatly to a curbing of the tendencies toward aestheticism among the followers of Nietzsche and provide a more balanced perspective on the modernity problematic.[24]

The issue of the relation of ethics and aesthetics continues to perplex the most nimble of inquiring minds and may indeed constitute one of the more thorny legacies of modernity. And a similar state of affairs obtains in the relation of the aesthetical and the ethical to the religious, which will enable us to open up a perspective on another dimension of self-understanding and self-constitution. Also, it will provide an occasion for addressing the Kierkegaard-effect in the shaping of the contours of the culture-spheres of modernity, requiring a consideration of religion as a culture-sphere along with the standard threesome of science, morality, and art.

At this juncture, however, the focus is specifically on the profile of the self in action, the self as actualized through choice and decision, the self as a project of unification amidst diversity striving for self-constancy and continuity. This profile of the self in action is of course to be understood in terms of its complementarity to the profile of the self in discourse. These profiles meet under the umbrella of communicative praxis, for the self that finds its origin as an implicature of communicative

24. A volume of collected essays on the contemporary relevance of the thought of Kierkegaard responds to the need for careful and critical studies on Kierkegaard's contribution to a multitude of issues dominating the current philosophical scene. See *Kierkegaard in Post/Modernity*, ed. Martin J. Matuštík and Merold Westphal (Bloomington: Indiana University Press, 1995).

praxis is an amalgam of discourse and action. Both the who of discourse and the who of action have much to do with temporality. The narrating self, as at once a sediment and a project of discourse, constitutes and understands itself as emplotted within the interstices of stories already told and stories yet to be inscribed. Likewise, the acting self is always embedded in social practices that reclaim a tradition and invoke a remembrance of things past in anticipation of future practices yet to be performed.

It is precisely this feature of the embeddedness of action in social practices that requires some attention. Certain limitations travel with the very grammar of "action" and "acting," limitations that have been intensified as a result of the specialization of the "philosophy of action" as a self-contained subdiscipline in the philosophy curriculum. When the circumscribed data for study in such a subdiscipline become discrete and insular bits of behavior—such as raising one's arm or flexing one's leg muscles—the stage is set for a pulverization of action into its abstracted components, a reification of the episodical, a separation of the elemental from the holistic background and context against which and in which the elemental units first take on sense and significance.

This tendency to pulverize the phenomenon of action into its discrete elemental units might appropriately be flagged as the predilection of an *abstract* empiricism, in which the experienced self and the experienced world are dissected into atomistic components that are then reified into insular and self-contained sense data. This abstract empiricism needs to be distinguished from *radical* empiricism as developed, for example, by William James. Radical empiricism furrows a more holistic and more consistently contextualized approach to experience. So as not to lose what James calls "the world as experienced" and the concrete experience of our embodiment as center of action within this wider world-experience, we need to be particularly attentive to the requirement for a reinsertion of any separately analyzable elements of action into higher-order configurations of social practices. And we shall use the grammar of *praxis,* which has found a rather prominent usage in the philosophical lexicon going all the way back to Aristotle in particular, to indicate the texture of these configurations of social practices in which human action unfolds and is understood.

The praxis in which particular actions are embedded encompasses not only a history of skills and techniques but also a background of habit formation, social customs, and institutional norms. Political negotiations, on both domestic and international fronts, provide telling illustrations of human action as at once individual and social. Julia Kristeva, in developing her notion of the subject-in-process, which she worked out consulting the twin contributions of linguistics and psychoanalysis, made it quite clear that any notion of self-constitution involves a politics of self-formation. She called this a politics of marginality because it appeals to resources of discourse and action as they take shape within the micropractices of marginalized groups in society. The main lesson to be learned from Kristeva's contribution is that any effort to sketch a portrait of the human self needs to move from purely semiotic or linguistic investigations to a psychology of motivation and action, and then to the wider economy of a polis in which the production and exchange of signs and the performance of individuated action first find their proper context for understanding and explanation.

To maximize concreteness in illustrating the relevance of the sociopolitical context for understanding and explaining human action, it might be helpful to develop a hermeneutical perspective on a specific event, which is itself composed of a series of events, in recent American diplomatic history. The negotiations by former president Jimmy Carter, retired general Colin

Powell, and Senator Sam Nunn with de facto president Emile Jonassaint and General Cédras on September 18, 1994, in connection with the crisis in Haiti, involved a peculiar mix of individual acts on the part of the negotiators with corporate action by political units. There was individual action in the exercise of bodily motility: Carter's folding his hands, Powell's shaking his finger, Cédras's shrugging his shoulders, and each man's grasping the pen in signing the accord. Now, each of these actions takes on sense and significance only against the backdrop of established social practices including techniques of persuasion, rules of political etiquette, and, most important, democratic processes in tension with procedures and policies of a military dictatorship. It is these social practices that limned the communicative praxis that was at issue in these negotiations, providing the social space in which the individual acts occurred, conferring upon them their contextualized meanings.

The placement of individual acts against the background of traditional and continuing social practices, reinserting them into the ongoing texture of communicative praxis, has the happy consequence of opening up a vision of the entwinement of discourse and action in the economy of public life. The example of political negotiation is particularly illustrative of this entwinement, for it displays at once a rhetoric of discourse and a rhetoric of action. Discourse, in the form of both the spoken and the written word, was in force during the negotiations. Indeed, newspaper accounts referred to the negotiations as "talks." One could thus speak of the accord that was reached as an achievement of discourse. But coupled with this rhetoric of discourse was an explicit rhetoric of action. Indeed, while the negotiations were in progress, planes loaded with American paratroopers were heading toward the Caribbean, warships began to close in on Haiti, and navy seals were making their way to the shores. In all this there was a display of a rhetoric of action, a nondiscursive form of persuasion that sent a message which in this situation may have been as consequential as that of the spoken and the written word.

The rhetoric scholar Kenneth Burke has developed a notion of "administrative rhetoric" that illustrates what I have in mind when I speak of a rhetoric of action. Burke defines administrative rhetoric as having to do with "persuasive devices which have a directly rhetorical aspect, yet include operations not confined to sheerly verbal persuasion." His example drawn from early twentieth-century American foreign policy is remarkably similar to my example of the rhetoric of action displayed in American foreign policy in more recent times. Burke's example is that of Theodore Roosevelt's sending the American fleet to the shores of Germany to pay the German emperor of the day the compliment of an allegedly friendly "goodwill mission—a goodwill visit or mission which was clearly rhetorical insofar as it was designed blandly to use a display of force as a mode of persuasion."[25] I find Burke's definition and example of admin-

25. Kenneth Burke, *Language as Symbolic Action* (Berkeley: University of California Press, 1968), p. 301. An original perspective on the role of rhetoric as it figures specifically in the odyssey of self-understanding has been developed by Ramsey Eric Ramsey and Lesley Di Mare. Experimenting with a critical continuation and refiguration of the Enlightenment uses of rationality, recalling Kant's linkage of genuine Enlightenment with individual and political freedom, Ramsey and Di Mare have devised a politics of critical rhetoric that pivots on the suggestive and promising distinction between *transforming* and *transformative* ideals. As transforming, ideals are textured in such a manner as to allow for change and evolution. They are transforming with respect to themselves, neither fixed nor foundational, and hence should be distinguished from traditional accounts of ideals as somehow universal and immutable. Ideals, however, are not simply *transforming;* they are also *transformative,* indicating their function in discourse and action as catalysts for effective sociopolitical change. See Ramsey Eric Ramsey, "Transversal Rationality, Rhetoric, and the Imagination: Probability and Contingency in

istrative rhetoric particularly helpful for highlighting the role of nondiscursive practices within the economy of communicative praxis, thus precluding a postmodern pantextualism that sees the world only through the lenses of textuality and discourse. Communicative praxis is both a discursive and nondiscursive affair, implicating and constituting the self as once speaking and acting subject, texturing the genealogy of self-formation as an adventure both in discourse and in action.

It is not unfortuitous that our discussion of the self in action has led us to conclude this chapter with a reference to rhetoric. Indeed, the self in its profiles of discourse and action is a rhetorical animal. In thus characterizing the self, we have the endorsement of at least one of the framers of Western philosophy, namely, Aristotle. Rhetoric, in Aristotle's book by that name, is defined as a *technē*, as an art and as a skill, as a performance of persuasion oriented toward action. But it is a technē that is not reducible to a calculating and controlling technique. More like a social practice than a technological tool, rhetoric for Aristotle is the art of persuasion, soliciting deliberation, choice, and action, oriented toward the projected good for the polis. Rhetoric is thus very much a *political* affair, but political in the sense of the Greek concept of the *polis*, which stands at the intersection of the interrelated notions of history, society, and community. In the next chapter we turn our attention to the bearing of these interrelated notions on the portrait of the self after postmodernity.

Experience and Judgment," in *Analecta Husserliana*, vol. 54, ed. A.-T. Tymieniecka (Dordrecht: Kluwer, 1996).

3

The Self in Community

An account of the self in action is destined to gravitate into an account of the self in community. The intentionality and intelligibility of particular human actions have their source in the social practices that structure the life of a given community. The term *praxis,* which has been in the philosophical vocabulary since the time of the Greeks, is particularly helpful for articulating the communal character of human existence. The parameters of the term extend to the skills, habits, customs, and public functions that provide the context of intelligibility for individuated bodily motility. And in pursuing that which praxis sets forth, one is led quite naturally to a recognition of the role of rhetoric, and more specifically to a rhetoric of communal action—which in turn brings to mind the contribution of Aristotle, who had already defined rhetoric as deliberation and action oriented toward that which is good for the polis, and who in his extensive discussions of the polis was wont to characterize man/woman as a political animal.

The Greek concept of the polis, however, is not isomorphic with the modern and postmodern concepts of the political, so some sorting is required. One needs to be particularly attentive to the polysemous vocabularies that have traveled with the concept of the polis throughout the ages, for example, society, socialization, state, government, civilization, and culture. In an effort to consolidate the polysemy and take up the slack in the range of multiple senses of the venerable concept of the polis, it would be advisable to experiment with the notions of "community," "communication," and more specifically "communicative praxis." To be sure, there is a rhetoric of community that carries admittedly problematic connotations. Some of these connotations make purchases on the preachments of a flaccid moralism that enjoins us to make the world a better place by learning to get along with each other. In a quite different vein, the grammar of community has been linked directly to a specific form of politico-economic organization, charging all those who express an interest in community with designs on the development of a communist state.

Recognizing these slippery slopes in the use of the notions of community and communication to flesh out some recoverable features of the ancient concept of the polis, and recognizing in addition that the historical context of the Greek polis is not that of the twentieth century, we nonetheless note that with the proper vigilance the polysemy that travels with the notion of community can direct us to the phenomenon of being-with-others. And it is against the backdrop of this phenomenon that one can bring into focus the contours of the third profile of the self after postmodernity—the self as discovering and constituting itself in relation to other selves.

The phenomenon of being-with-others has already been noted in the previous two chapters, albeit somewhat obliquely. The self that is called into being through discourse and action is at the same time called into being within a community. This was already announced in the recurring references to communicative praxis as an amalgam of discourse and action, supplying the textured space for the self-implicature of the human subject in its manifold concretions. The present task is to render explicit the communicative feature of this space, in which discourse and action move about. The shift to the phenomenon of being-with-others as the source and dynamic of community will also provide an opportunity to respond to the postmodern challenge as it pertains to the accentuation of alterity in its multiple guises.

The central project in this chapter is to address the issue of community as it arises from the phenomenon of being-with-others and shows itself in a concrete "we-experience," in which the "I-experience" of the who of discourse and the who of action is recursively activated. The format proceeds from an examination of the we-experience within the density of face-to-face encounters to its posture within the wider sociopolitical arena of institutional involvement and communal action, and then to its function within a global historicity. As in the previous chapters, a progressive deconstruction of the Cartesian ego-cogito remains in force, salvaging Descartes's existential interest in the who of the subject while dismantling the official Cartesian concept of mind. In sketching the profile of the self in action, we recommended a reanalysis of the celebrated "I think, therefore I am" into the semantics of "I choose, therefore I am." In probing the phenomenon of the self in community, we propose a continuation of our deconstructive redescription, submitting to our interlocutors that "We interact, therefore we are." It is in community that the thinking, speaking, and acting by the subject undergo a conjunctive synthesis. Jean-Luc Nancy, in addressing the question "Who comes after the subject?" and in particular after the subject as a Cartesian thinking substance, responds with a telling question of his own: "*Who* thinks, if not the community?"[1] Community is constitutive of selfhood. It fleshes out the portrait of the self by engendering a shift of focus from the self as present to itself to the self as present *to, for,* and *with* the other.

1. Eduardo Cadava, Peter Connor, and Jean-Luc Nancy, eds., *Who Comes After the Subject?* (New York: Routledge, 1991), p. 8.

It is common in the current literature to indict the proponents of postmodernism, and particularly the representatives of the French persuasion, for being unable to say "we." Such is the case, for example, in Richard Rorty's swipe at the discourses of Michel Foucault and other current French philosophers. The discourses of Foucault, according to Rorty, are characterized by a "dryness produced by a lack of identification with any social context, any communication. Foucault once said that he would like to write 'as to have no face.' He forbids himself the tone of the liberal sort of thinker who says to his fellow-citizens: 'We know that there must be a better way to do things than this; let us look for it together.' There is no 'we' to be found in Foucault's writings, nor in those of many of his French contemporaries."[2] Although Rorty's critical assessment of Foucault's inability to come to terms with the phenomenon of the we-experience may be somewhat overextended, it is difficult to situate any positive role for community within the parameters of postmodern discourse. Any effort to sketch a portrait of the self after postmodernity will thus need to give particular attention to this issue. And in the end we may discover that if we cannot find a proper setting for the we-experience, then the location of the I-experience will also elude us.

The we-experience and the I-experience are more intricately entwined than has been acknowledged by proponents of either the social doctrine of the self or the individualist doctrine. Whereas the social doctrine defines the self as simply an ensemble and product of societal relations, the individualist perspective argues for a self-constituting individuality that proceeds independently of relations with other selves. The first

2. Richard Rorty, "Habermas and Lyotard on Postmodernity," in *Habermas and Modernity*, ed. Richard J. Bernstein (Cambridge: MIT Press, 1985), p. 172.

doctrine buys into a species of collectivism and a semblance of group substantiality, relegating the individual qua individual to the status of a societal epiphenomenon. The other doctrine makes purchases on an egology, of either an empirical or a transcendental sort, and locates the primary datum of selfhood in a sphere of ownness that antedates the acknowledgment of other egos. The point is that both these doctrines trade on a common mistake of sundering an undivided portion of the world-experience and then reifying the abstracted components. Sociologism and egologism alike are unacceptable alternatives for elucidating the portrait of the self as human subject.

Elucidations of the phenomenon of being-with-others as it unfolds in the concrete we-experience have been particularly vulnerable to the intrusions of grand theorizing decked out with elaborate scaffoldings of social construction. The penchant for theoretical construction has been particularly noticeable in the history of the human sciences. From scientific Marxism with its inexorable laws of class struggle to structuralism with its synchronic infrastructural relations to Habermas's philosophy of communicative action and his fascination with systems theory, much of recent social philosophy has followed the path of theory construction in the grand style. This is why the study by the African American philosopher Lewis R. Gordon on the crises of concepts in the human sciences is such a welcome corrective to a social theorizing that loses its way in the conceptual labyrinths of societal constructs. Although not disdainful of social theory per se, Gordon takes particular care to keep theoretical ruminations rooted in what he calls "embodied agency."[3] In his close analysis and description of embodied agency as

3. Lewis R. Gordon, *Fanon and the Crisis of European Man: An Essay on Philosophy and the Human Sciences* (New York: Routledge, 1995). See particularly chap. 3, "Racism, Colonialism, and Anonymity: Social Theory and Embodied Agency," pp. 37–66.

at once catalyst and goal for social change and reconstruction, Gordon is able to articulate the dialectical entwinement of bodily self-identity with cultural formation. The phenomenon of the social is understood neither by consulting a registry of methodological matrices nor by cataloguing the newest contributions by systems theory, but rather through a disciplined investigation of the struggles of embodied agents seeking liberation and recognition in a concrete lifeworld of confrontation and participation.

The story of the struggle of embodied agents, as narrated by Gordon, unfolds against the backdrop of a history of being-with-others infected with the dehumanizing threats of racism and colonialism. The hero in this story of the fight against the depersonalization of the we-experience is Frantz Fanon, at once philosopher, psychiatrist, and key figure in the Algerian National Liberation Front during the mid-twentieth century. It was Fanon's provocative essay *The Wretched of the Earth* that quickened the conscience of the world by calling attention to the traumatization of a minority people by an oppressive regime.[4] Making use of Jean-Paul Sartre's existential analysis of bad faith, Gordon provides a trenchant explication of the racism and colonialism against which Fanon struggled during his lifetime. What one learns from the story that Gordon tells so well is that in the polis of the twentieth century the phenomenon of being-with-others, in the originative sense of *phenomenon* as "that which shows itself," indeed shows itself in sundry times and places under the conditions of alienation and estrangement. Recalling Hegel's celebrated assessment that history is not a "theatre of happiness," we do well to remember that the twentieth century, contrary to the dreams and expecta-

4. Frantz Fanon, *The Wretched of the Earth,* trans. Constance Farrington (New York: Grove Press, 1963).

tions of the philosophers of the Age of Enlightenment, has not achieved perfection in its struggles for personal freedom and social harmony.

Any sketching of the profile of the self in community will thus need to begin with a full recognition of the discourse and action of embodied agents, face-to-face in situations of agreement and dissent, harmony and discord, liberation and oppression, mastery and slavery. In search of an appropriate beginning, in full awareness that all beginnings are contingent and that wherever one stands one's discourse and action has already begun, we select as an opener for our account of the self in community the simple question, "Who is the other self that I encounter in my dealings with the world?" In my everyday preoccupations, at work and at play, I meet other selves. I look up and see them; I greet them; I shake their hands; I recall having met them before; I return their friendly smiles or recoil from their intimidating stares; I recognize them as stranger or acquaintance, as liberator or oppressor. I discern their situation in life and social role to be that of friend or foe, citizen or alien, employer or employee, doctor or patient, lawyer or client—and the list of putative roles and functions goes on. What is it that transpires in the meeting of self with other self? What dynamic of intentionality is operative in the face-to-face encounter with another person? What sense can we ascribe to the "otherness" of the other person *as other* in the multiple modalities of his or her self-presentation?

Although these questions have received the attention of philosophical minds since the beginnings of occidental thought, it is particularly since the advent of modern philosophy that they have congealed into a thorny philosophical problem. Much of this had to do with the epistemological turn to the subject as this turn was maneuvered by the father of modern philosophy, René Descartes. If the only legitimate starting point and stable foundation for knowledge is the existence of an ego-cogito as self-contained and insular mental substance, then all avenues toward knowledge of other egos become problematized and the specters of skepticism and solipsism appear on the horizon. Grappling with the problem of the existence of other minds thus became one of the more time-consuming tasks in post-Cartesian philosophy, both on the Continent and in Great Britain. The feverish pursuit of an incorrigible knowledge of other minds congealed into a distinguishing mark of modernity and reached an epistemological stalemate in the philosophical skepticism of David Hume.

A breakthrough of sorts in the framing of the problem occurred in the development of phenomenology by the German philosopher Edmund Husserl in his important work *Cartesian Meditations*. Husserl's phenomenology, as an investigation of *meaning* geared toward an analysis of *phenomena* defined as "objects-as-meant," focused not on the existence-problem pertaining to other egos but rather sought clarification of the meaning of the otherness of the other self *as other*. The phenomenological analysis of the constitution of the meaning of alterity in our experience of other selves, carried through by Husserl in *Meditation* V, is at once brilliant and profound. But for all that, the results of his explorations and analyses, as subsequent interpreters and critics of Husserl were not long in pointing out, fell short of resolving the problem. And this was the case primarily because his project remained within the constraints of a "Cartesian meditation" on the issue at hand. Although he had jettisoned the Cartesian metaphysical doctrine of the self as a mental substance, Husserl continued the inquiry from the standpoint of a foundationalist subjectivity, addressing the question about the other self from the perspective of analogical attributes that proceed from a prior translucent understanding of the self as founding subject. But within such a scheme of things the most that can be achieved is an understanding of the other as other-for-me, the other as alter ego, constituted through an analogical pairing and projection. It is our considered judgment, however, that an understanding of the otherness of the other, remains on the hither side of any constitutive analogical projection issuing from a centered subject.

What is required is a decentering of any putatively centered ego, including the phenomenological version, as part of the continuing project of deconstructing the Cartesian doctrine of a sovereign subject. And this is required specifically so as to make possible the advential or supervenient presence of the other—the other not simply as other-for-me but as staking an ontological claim on my own subjectivity. The otherness of the other needs be granted its intrinsic integrity, so that in seeing the face of the other and hearing the voice of the other I am *responding* to an exterior gaze and an exterior voice rather than carrying on a conversation with my alter ego. I do not create the discourse and the action of others. I encounter the entwined discourse and action of the other and respond to it, and in this encountering and responding I effect a self-constitution, a constitution of myself, in the dynamic economy of being-with-others.

In addressing the issue of the self in community it thus behooves us to begin with a clear recognition that the phenomenon of being-with-others in its multiple modalities suffers the insinuations of alterity. This phenomenon cannot be reduced to the dispositions, intentions, and projects of the experiencing subject. In a manner reminiscent of Kant, we can say that knowledge of the other self *begins* with experience, but then we must quickly add—as did Kant but for different reasons—that our knowledge of the other self does not *arise out* of experience. Knowledge of the other as other arises out of exterior and supervenient forces that impinge or intrude on our experience—forces issuing from visages, voices, and actions always already extant. This is most poignantly the case when these visages, voices, and actions are signals and cries of discontent, oppression, and suffering.

We alluded to the announcement of such voices and embodied actions within the economy of being-with-others in the reference to Frantz Fanon's encounter with racism and colonialism. A complementing story of the alterity of voices, visages, and action during seasons of discontent in modern civilization is told by the French philosopher Emmanuel Levinas. Fanon and Levinas, as, respectively, a black facing the racism of an oppressive colonialism and a Jew experiencing the demonic consequences of the Holocaust, were peculiarly well positioned to address the profound ambiguities that reside in the polis of the twentieth century. Some of these ambiguities are given specific attention in Levinas's ethics of alterity, in which the other is able to assume the voice and visage of the teacher issuing the commandment "Thou shalt not kill" and then metamorphose into the voice of the executioner, countermand the commandment, and assume the role of the exterminator in the interests of ethnic cleansing. Although the otherness of the other stands out most sharply in the accounts of extreme cases of racism, political oppression, and religious persecution, the facticity of otherness pervades our everyday coming and going forth as we encounter the stranger in our midst, meet the orphan, look at the face of the grieving widow, and hear the laments of the economically disenfranchised.[5]

One thus does well to approach the topic of the self in community by attending to the phenomenon of being-with-

5. See particularly Emmanuel Levinas, *Totality and Infinity*, trans. Alphonso Lingis (Pittsburgh: Duquesne University Press, 1996), sec. 3, "Exteriority and the Face."

others in the modality of face-to-face encounters, as these encounters eventuate in perception and action, in dialogue and in discord, in enjoyment and in suffering. We need to exercise some caution, however, to avoid having being-with-the-other in the concreteness of the one-to-one relationship or disrelationship become an isolated phenomenon, a circumscribed social fact exhibiting a self-contained locus of meaning. Being-with-the-other takes on meaning only against the backdrop of wider historico-cultural forces of self and societal formation. Just as events of discourse and action require for their intelligibility an insertion into the history of discursive and institutional practices, so also the face-to-face encounters of the self with the other take on meaning only against the background of a tradition already delivered and the foreground of one yet to be enacted. It is this historical perspective that provides the proper space and parameters for the self in community. Self-understanding entails an understanding of oneself as a citizen of a polis, a player in an ongoing tradition of beliefs and commitments, a participant in an expanding range of institutions and traditions.

Because of the slackness in the grammar of ordinary usage, we have thus far permitted the notions of community and society to slide into one another as they play in the wider polis of human relations. But now that we have moved into considerations of a more encompassing historical perspective with its insinuation of background beliefs and practices, it is necessary to consolidate some of our vocabulary about the polis, both ancient and modern. Only by doing so will we see our way clear as we move through the multiplicity of converging and conflicting traditions with their variegated contributions in the culture-spheres of science, morality, art, and religion.

Against this backdrop of contextualized historical and cultural developments, the need to distinguish between community and society would appear to be of particular consequence. To view the self as called into being through community and communication extends the sense of simply being in society. Discourse and action are already thoroughly socialized. Clearly, being-with-the-other is a *social* event, but socialization does not by itself contain the significations that we find associated with *community*. Discourse and action gather social predicates as they traffic in the affairs of customs and conventions of everyday life, but community is more than customs and conventions of the tradition. Community is more like the binding textuality of our discourse and the integrating purpose of our action. Community, reminiscent of the ancient Greek concept of the polis, takes on a determination of value and is indicative of an ethico-moral dimension of human life.

During the early twentieth century, John Dewey, addressing the effects of industrialization within the fabric of society, was motivated to distinguish social institutions and technological progress from that which informs a sense of community. "The Great Society created by steam and electricity may be a society, but it is no community," observes Dewey. He continues, "The invasion of the community by new and relatively impersonal and mechanical modes of combined behavior is the outstanding fact of modern life."[6] What Dewey here recognizes, and what

6. John Dewey, *The Public and Its Problems* (New York: Holt, 1929), p. 98. Other philosophers roughly within the same time frame expressed concerns similar to Dewey's about public life in the modern world. Already in the mid-nineteenth century, Karl Marx in his *Economic and Philosophic Manuscripts of 1844* addressed the widespread alienation of the worker from his work, from other workers, and ultimately from himself. The existentialist philosopher Karl Jaspers, in his small volume *Man in the Modern Age*, first published in 1931, wrote of a "technical mass-order" in which "the masses are our masters" and we have been constrained "to become as automatic as ants" (trans. Eden and Cedar Paul [Garden City, N.J.: Doubleday Anchor Books, 1957], p. 40). Jaspers's French counter-

others have also recognized, is that "community" is not a pure, value-free description of a societal state of affairs. The very notion of a communal being-with-others is linked to normative and evaluative signifiers. This should come as no surprise, because the discourse that is operative in the process of self-formation is a mixed discourse, in which the descriptive and the prescriptive, the denotative and the evaluative, commingle and become entwined. One of the tasks of philosophical analysis is to monitor the effects of this commingling and entwinement on the project of self-understanding within a communal existence.

As the grammar of community falls out as a mixed discourse of the descriptive and the prescriptive, so is this also the case with the grammars of the more or less value-free notions of society, sociality, and socialization. There is no purely descriptive fact of being-with, no value-neutral intersubjective state of affairs. The "sociality" of being-with is always already oriented either toward a creative and life-affirming intersubjectivity or toward a destructive and life-negating mode of being-with-others. It is thus that one is able to define community as principally a creative and self-affirming modality of being-with-others in society, as contrasted with conformism and mere conventionalism as a self-effacing modality of being-with. Community and conformity are alternative modalities of being with other selves. And as being-alone is a mode of being complementing that of being-with, we need to speak of analogous modalities of being-alone. We find these in solitude, properly

part Gabriel Marcel, in his *Man Against Mass Society* (trans. G. S. Fraser [Chicago: Henry Regnery, 1962]) made much of the loss of selfhood through a reduction of the human subject to an assemblage of functions. And Martin Heidegger in his assorted writings highlighted the threats of technologization to our efforts at understanding ourselves and our world.

understood as a creative way of being-alone, contrasted with loneliness, as a self-destructive modality of being-alone.[7]

It is this mixed discourse of description and prescription, denotation and evaluation, as it pertains to our being-with and being-alone, that needs to be monitored and that has received some attention from contemporary ethicists and social philosophers. Charles Taylor, representing the Anglo-American tradition on the issues at hand, and Jürgen Habermas, representing the continental tradition (and more specifically the School of Critical Theory), are cases in point.

Taylor, in his 1989 work *Sources of the Self: The Making of Modern Identity*, addresses the issue of selfhood from two intercalating perspectives and strands of reflection. The first perspective is oriented toward a description of who we are; the other probes the meaning and worth of our lives. Questions concerning personal identity intersect issues having to do with the moral life of humankind. It is Taylor's view that in order to achieve an understanding of what it means to be a human subject one has to intertwine the topic of personal identity with considerations of what constitutes the good life. And this questioning by the self vis-à-vis its relation to the good can proceed, according to Taylor, only in recognition of the self's interdependence with other selves. The self's understanding and actualization of that which is good for it is always embedded in forms of discourse and projects of action that testify to the involvements with other selves. Each individual, avers Taylor, "may take up a stance which is authentically his or her own; but the

7. One might speculate that considerations of this sort motivated A. N. Whitehead to define religion in relation to solitude: "Religion is what the individual does with his own solitariness" (*Religion in the Making* [New York: Meridian Books, 1960], p. 16).

very possibility of this is enframed in a social understanding of great temporal depth, in fact, in a 'tradition.'"[8] It is thus that questions of personal identity and moral worth mix and mingle, as do issues of personal actualization and communal interdependence, indicating that any philosophy of the self will at the same time be a philosophy of society and community.

Jürgen Habermas's approach to the issues at hand exhibits concerns similar to those of Taylor; however, Habermas makes a more aggressive move in the direction of social theorizing. His massive two-volume work *The Theory of Communicative Action* provides a multi-tiered social philosophy that proceeds "with the systematic aim of laying out the problems that can be solved by means of a theory of rationalization developed in terms of the basic concept of communicative action. What can lead us to this goal is not a history of ideas but a history of theory with systemic intent."[9] What this encompassing historical and systematic project of social theory purports to deliver in the end is nothing less than a resolution of the problem of modernity, defined as the recalcitrant diremption of the culture-spheres of science, morality, and art. Part of the task in effecting the unification of the differentiated culture-spheres, as envisioned by Habermas, is showing how the validity claims in the "truth" of propositions are able to connect with the validity claims of "rightness" in regard to normative obligations, thanks to an underbelly of communicative rationality that informs and binds the culture-spheres of the cognitive-instrumental (the descriptive) and the moral-practical (the prescriptive). Although in the final analysis Habermas's grand theory of communicative

8. Charles Taylor, *Sources of the Self: The Making of Modern Identity* (Cambridge: Harvard University Press, 1989), p. 39.

9. Jürgen Habermas, *The Theory of Communicative Action*, vol. 1, trans. Thomas McCarthy (Boston: Beacon Press, 1984), pp. 139–140.

action is not Taylor's perspective on the historically and culturally indexed self (nor is it my own analysis and interpretation of the structure and dynamics of communicative praxis), what these views call to our attention is that any portrait of the human self will need to recognize the sociohistorical sources of self-constitution and the unavoidability of ethico-moral considerations.

The profile of the self in community that is proffered in this chapter is designed to accommodate both of these requirements—recognizing the historical and cultural features of self-constitution while attending to the ethico-moral fabric of self-actualization—through a play with the operative notions of *responsivity* and *responsibility*. Responsivity functions basically as a descriptive term; responsibility connotes, if not an explicitly prescriptive content, in a significant measure an ethical stance, an ethos, a way of dwelling in a social world that gives rise to human goals and purposes, obligations, duties, and concerns for human rights.

Throughout the preceding discussions a point that has been given particular emphasis is that the discourse and action that play such prominent roles in the process of self-formation are always a discourse and action responding to prior discourse and prior action. Hence the parameters for any socialization of the self have already been marked out. Within these parameters the self never begins itself; it finds itself to be always already begun. And it is always already begun by virtue of its responsivity to the speech and action of others. The current task is to provide an account of the conversion of responsivity into responsibility, the move from a state of affairs of being-with-others to the insinuation of ethico-moral requirements to respond in a fitting manner. The ability to respond, being able to respond, becomes aligned with a moral injunction to do so in the proper way. It is this that we understand by the phenomenon of responsibility—

being responsible in our responding to prior action upon us—and it is this phenomenon that provides the space for what might appropriately be called the "ethic of the fitting response."

Before proceeding with an unpacking of the dynamics of the fitting response as it plays itself out in the profile of the self in community, we need to address the issue of the transition from descriptive responsivity to normative responsibility, from what one might call the fact of being-with-others to the value of being-with-others in a certain manner. This issue needs to be addressed because of the long-standing philosophical predilection to dichotomize facts and values, descriptions and prescriptions, states of affairs and norms. One of the pressing requirements of the times is to problematize this received predilection.

The descriptive and the prescriptive envelop each other in the economy of the mixed discourse of everyday usage. A description of the state of affairs in regard to overpopulation is also a normative judgment that issues a call for social change and political action. Resistance to a network of power relations in a given segment of society travels with at least an implicit normative claim that such resistance should be undertaken. When my wife tells me that the garbage smells, the constative is also an injunction to take the trash out. This all attests to the slippery signifiers in our grammar of "fact." Indeed, we have invited a species of philosophical bamboozlement because of a hurried acceptance of an "atomic" or "bare-bones" theory of fact. This is the theory that facts are brute givens, somehow simply there, data that we stumble on like pebbles on the beach. This theory, which is basically a construct of an abstract empiricism, should be jettisoned, and attention should be shifted to what it is that goes on in the actual practice of scientific and philosophical inquiry. What we find in such inquiry is that facts do not fall from heaven as insular and discrete entities but are rather *constituted as facts* within a variety of disciplinary matrices. A fact, whether physical or social, *becomes* a fact when it is *taken as* being relevant for the inquiry at hand. This taking something as something flags the interpretive moment in our inquiry into facts. There are no facts without interpretation. And interpretation is always the work of a *community* of interpreters, as the American philosopher Charles Sanders Peirce had demonstrated at some length.

Facts thus become defined as facts only against the backdrop of communalized interpretive practices. But such is also the case with respect to values. Values, like facts, do not fall fully clothed, fixed and finished, from some celestial abode. Values become values only when they are *taken as* being valuable within the concrete context of everyday life. Like facts, values are constituted and defined against the backdrop of communalized interpretive practices. These interpretive practices provide the space from which knowledge and valuation, descriptive properties and ethical assessments, emerge. Facts and values alike are Johnnies-come-lately, secondary and derivative, emergent from what one might call a third dimension, a dimension of lived-through processes of individual, institutional, and cultural formation.

It is in this third dimension, the dimension of the everyday and concretely experienced lifeworld, the dimension of ordinary discourse and practical dealings, antedating the derivation of facts and values, that we find a phenomenon that plays a pivotal role for the ethical requirement. This is the phenomenon of conscience, which has been given widespread treatment in the history of religion, literature, and philosophy, but which for all that still remains an opaque and elusive though indispensable condition for ethico-moral experience. A clarification of the workings of conscience will require an articulation of its role in dealing with the delivered habits, customs, and conventions that make up the culture-forms in the life of the individual and the life of society. Conscience is, if you will, the catalyst of critique for addressing modes of ethical behavior, accepting some while rejecting others, and calling for changes in one's personal life and in the public sphere. It is conscience that informs us about the misdeeds and misdirections in the way we conduct our lives and that tells us there is a better way to do things. But it is precisely the genealogy of conscience, its source and dynamics, that occasions a measure of puzzlement. Whence the call of conscience and whither its disposition? Does the call simply issue from sedimented moral sanctions, taboos and prescriptions ensconced in the cultural history of the race? Is its voice simply that of introjected authority figures, the repressive norms of a superego? Or does the voice of conscience issue a call to an authentic self-being, to a courage to be oneself amid the threats of conformism and conventionalism, and to a motivation for redress of social ills in public life?

It was particularly the repressive and leveling function of conscience that concerned Nietzsche (as it did of course also Sigmund Freud) and inspired Nietzsche's diatribe against the "good" and "bad" conscience as no more than an instrument of herd morality in which the individual is subordinated to the stultifying and enervating mores of the public. This subordination of the individual, through a repressive functioning of conscience, can indeed lead to a virtual displacement of the individuality of the individual, as in the case of the frightening declaration by Hermann Goering, "I have no conscience. The Führer is my conscience." Heidegger addresses a similar predicament, but with a more positive understanding of the role and function of conscience, when he portrays the call of conscience as a liberating voice, calling *Dasein* out of the dictatorship of *das man*, the phenomenon of the "they-self" or the "anonymous one," which is basically the self in subjugation to customary and conventional discourse and action. And the call of conscience as a freeing of the self *from* the dictatorship of *das man* is at once a call *to* and *for* an authentic existence, crowned by resolute choice and action. One of the more significant moments in the scenario of the call of conscience as portrayed by Heidegger is the recognition that heeding the call is both an individual task and a social responsibility in which the individuated *Dasein* faces the other, and it faces the other *either* in the unauthentic mode of conventionalism, mass hysteria, and the superimposition of ideology, *or* in the authentic mode of creative intersubjective self-actualization.[10]

This peculiar status and function of conscience, as defined by Heidegger as a call out of a flattened and depersonalized existence to the authenticity of resolute responsibility, requires some critical assessment. The Heideggerian conscience is transmoral in character, as is also the resolve (*Entschlossenheit*) to which it calls us. Like Nietzsche's will-to-power, Heidegger's resolute existence is situated "beyond good and evil." Hence, the question "Wherein resides the authority and the moral sanction of conscience?" receives no answer within the designs of Heidegger's ontological analytic. Questions of morality are for Heidegger ontic considerations, and he makes it quite clear that the ontic is not to be taken for the ontological. Yet, from this it does not follow that the question about the authority and moral sanction of conscience is to be ruled out of court. Indeed, Heidegger could have addressed the issue, given his intermittent reminders that the ontological is rooted (*verwurzelt*) in the

10. For a particularly incisive analysis of Heidegger's concept of conscience as it relates specifically to the task and function of rhetoric see Michael J. Hyde, "The Call of Conscience: Heidegger and the Question of Rhetoric," *Philosophy and Rhetoric,* vol. 27, no. 4, 1994. In this article Hyde develops a sustained discussion of how the call of conscience, as understood by Heidegger, calls for the building of community through the practice of rhetoric.

ontic. But the fact remains that he did not address the issue, and this may raise some questions about the practical cash value of an ontological analytic that furrows a labyrinth on the hither side of the distinction between good and evil.

To place the question about the integrative authority of conscience into a promising perspective, one would do well to recall the contribution of one of the more neglected philosophers in the history of moral philosophy, Joseph Butler. Usually classified as a representative of the "moral sense" approach to ethical theory, Butler found conscience to be the pivotal, organizing, and directing principle for the moral sense. As the crowning faculty in Butler's doctrine of human nature, taking precedence over the subordinate faculties and functions of the appetites, self-love, and benevolence, conscience enjoys an authoritative role in the legislation of the moral life. The authority and sanction of conscience as the guide for life resides within its performance as a "superior principle of reflection."[11] It is this linkage of conscience and reflection that provides Butler's theory of conscience with its distinctive stamp, and it is this linkage that clears the path for addressing the question as to the authority and sanction of the moral sense.

As a reflective rational principle, conscience is not to be confused with the nonreflective authoritarian conscience that is simply the voice of custom and convention. Conscience, for Butler, is not simply a motivating factor, a propensity, a vector of force, a dynamic principle. To be sure, it *is* a dynamic principle, but one that carries a cognitive sanction. Now, it may indeed be the case that the reflective principle that Butler integrated into the workings of conscience is too cognitive-theoretical in design. Butler, however, was one of the few think-

11. Joseph Butler, *The Works of Joseph Butler,* vol. 2, *Fifteen Sermons on Human Nature* (Oxford: Clarendon Press, 1986), p. 59.

ers of his age to come upon the insight that conscience is a mode of moral understanding; a manner of knowing one's way about in moral predicaments; a practical wisdom of what the situation requires, given the potentialities and constraints of our human nature.

To forestall an overly cognitivist reading of Butler's principle of reflection, one would do well to experiment with an analysis of reflection into *discernment*—a discernment that provides its own criterion for judgment, through praxis-oriented understanding. And we have David James Miller to thank for tracing this praxis-grounded notion of criterion back to the ancient Greek usage of *krino*, which in its polysemous employment expressed the interrelated senses of discerning, distinguishing, picking out, judging, and assessing.[12] What is at issue here is the observation, apparently going all the way back to the origins of the Western tradition, that there is a praxis-imbued discernment, a practical reasoning and reflection, that provides its own insight and sanction for moral judgments. The performance of this discernment, as Wittgenstein took pains to show, is visible in the ordinary usages of our multiple language games through which we classify, discriminate, and identify objects and states of affairs by marking out differences. This construal of discernment as supplying its own criterion and sanction for judgment antedates, both historically and epistemologically, the modern rule-governed, criteriological conception of rationality, which would have us lay down the criteria for judgment in advance and then legislate rules for guiding us to the citadel of certain knowledge.

The lesson to be learned from our brief excursus into Butler's understanding of conscience as a principle of reflection,

12. David James Miller, "Immodest Interventions," *Phenomenological Inquiry*, vol. 2, October 1987, p. 109.

and from our analysis of reflection into a more praxis-imbued discernment, is that conscience is able to supply the requisite authority and direction for responsible moral deliberation and action within the community of actors.[13] It is thus that the dynamics and discernment of conscience stimulate the economy of what I have named the third dimension, the situated configurations of our mixed discourse and lived-through experience that antedates the split between abstracted facts and values and provides the praxial space for infusing responsivity with responsibility, giving birth to the self as ethically defined.

So we come to speak of an ethic of the fitting response in fleshing out the profile of the self in the community. In a previous work the services of the Greek concept of *kathakonta,* "the fitting," were solicited to further an understanding of the ethical requirement of the self in community.[14] To exist ethically with other selves is to respond in a fitting manner to their discourse and action. It is important, however, not to confuse the fitting response with simple accommodation. To respond in a

13. An issue that arises in Butler's moral sense theory of conscience — and which may well be an issue germane to all notions of conscience — is whether the authority and sanction of conscience is somehow self-authenticating. Admittedly, as a cleric Butler saw conscience to be a gift of God. It is in conscience that the voice of God can be heard. This, of course, provides conscience with an even greater aura of authority and moral certainty. Butler, however, was of the mind that the sanction and integrative function of conscience could be established independent of theological sanctions. To what extent he was successful in defending his justification for the moral sanction of conscience on the basis of purely philosophical considerations remains one of the moot questions in the history of moral philosophy. For a helpful discussion of this issue see Stephen C. Pepper, *Ethics* (New York: Appleton-Century-Crofts, 1960), pp. 238–247.

14. Calvin O. Schrag, *Communicative Praxis and the Space of Subjectivity* (Bloomington: Indiana University Press, 1986). See particularly pt. 3, chap. 10, "Ethos, Ethics, and a New Humanism."

fitting manner is not simply to accommodate oneself to that which is going on. It involves discernment, evaluation, critical judgment—what we have come to call "praxial critique." For a response to be fitting it may require a radical revision of an established custom or convention, or indeed its overturn.[15] I am indebted to John M. Fritzman for highlighting the moment of critical agency in my understanding and use of the notion of the fitting response by pointing out the important difference between my position and that of Gadamer. Fritzman correctly notes that both Gadamer and I are interested in reclaiming certain insights from the Greek concept of phronesis as practical wisdom. Whereas Gadamer restricts practical wisdom to a discernment and application of criteria that are already constituted by and remain immanent in the delivered tradition, my notion of the fitting response allows for a more explicit distanciation from and intervention into the tradition. "At their most daring—for example, in Hans-Georg Gadamer's work on *phronesis*—such interpretations at best allow that the delivered tradition also immanently contains the resources for discerning aspects of the criteria which always were present, but not detected hitherto. On Schrag's account, however, *it is the intervention itself that retroactively constitutes the delivered traditions which will provide backdrops to the intervention!* It is the subject's encounters with the other which establish the contexts of those encounters. It is for this reason that the judgment regarding the fittingness of an intervention always is a matter of hindsight. This judgment always occurs in the intervention's future, and is

15. For a discussion of the conditions and dynamics of praxial critique and the connection of such praxial critique with criteria see Calvin O. Schrag, *The Resources of Rationality: A Response to the Postmodern Challenge* (Bloomington: Indiana University Press, 1992), chap. 2, "Rationality as Praxial Critique."

itself another intervention. It should be obvious that the fitting response is an active—and not a reactive—force."[16]

Responsibility, nurtured by the call of conscience, supplies the moral dimension in the narrative of the self in community. To be in community is to recognize the requirement not only to respond to prior discourse and action but to respond in a fitting manner. In heeding the call of conscience, one is always directed to the voice and the face of the other, and this other is always a resident in an exterior space. No longer an alter ego, issuing from the depths of subjectivity, the other displays an integrity and existential resiliency, advential and supervenient. On this point it is prudent to side with Levinas rather than with Hegel, avowing an original asymmetry within the self-other relation. The radical exteriority of the other as other needs to be acknowledged, attested, and assented to—and it is in this acknowledging, attesting, and assenting that the genealogy of ethics finds its source. This constitutes the ethical moment, in which one understands oneself as a self-in-community, implicated in an acknowledgment of an other who is not of one's making, and to whose voice and action one is called upon to respond in a fitting manner.

The analysis of responsibility into an ethic of the fitting response, it needs to be emphasized, is not to be understood as another piece of ethical theory, alongside teleological, deontological, and utilitarian theories. One of the problems in the study of ethics in departments of philosophy in sundry colleges and universities is the compartmentalization of ethics as a self-contained subdiscipline, geared to an excessive preoccupation with the theoretical—as though we were in dire need of

16. John M. Fritzman, "The Future of Nostalgia and the Time of the Sublime," *CLIO: A Journal of Literature, History and the Philosophy of History,* vol. 23, no. 2, 1994, p. 185.

yet another theory of moral obligation, another platform of re-treaded universal or quasi-universal ethico-moral principles, to back up the discernment and evaluation that is always already in force in our concrete and specific communicative practices. Just as one finds the specialized discipline of epistemology to exude a measure of philosophical incoherence in its effort to solve the problem of the knowledge of knowledge, so one would be well advised to consider theorizing about the ethical to be an elusive search for a foundationalist justification of how we are to live our lives.

The characterization of the ethical as being composed of fitting responses within the context of community has been designed to call attention to ethics as a praxis rather than an inventory of theoretically grounded principles. The ethical has to do with *ethos* in its orginative sense of a cultural dwelling, a mode or manner of historical existence, a way of being in the world that exhibits a responsibility both to oneself and to others. It is this that defines the bearing of the self as ethical subject, whose subjectivity is always that of an intersubjectivity. This portrait of the ethical subject needs to be distinguished both from the classical metaphysical theory of the self as a soul-substance and from modern formal and empirical theories of the self as moral agent. In such portraits the self is prejudged as an entity of sorts—substantial, formal, or empirical—to which moral predicates and value properties might then be assigned. Consequently, the ethical subject is viewed as a peculiar entity (as either a ghost in a machine or a machine without a ghost) that happens to *have or possess* certain moral properties or value attributes. It is this conceptual framework and grammar of attributes, properties, and predicates, couched in metaphors of possession, that is found to be so problematic in an inquiry into the being and behavior of the ethical subject. Within such a framework of consumerist morality the economy of the ethical self is driven by the desire to accumulate more and more moral properties, progressively expanding, as it were, its moral curriculum vita. The displacement of this framework enables one to view the self as ethical not because it has managed to collect and accumulate abstractive attributes, properties, and predicates, but instead because it *exists ethically*—and to exist ethically is to respond to the prior discourse and action of other selves within the constraints of a communal world.

Our sketch of the profile of the self in community thus culminates in a delineation of the ethical as a fitting response to the alterity of the discourse and the action of those with whom the self shares a concrete lifeworld. This delineation clearly places a premium on the contextuality and contingency of local and historically specific social practices. But does this not threaten the validity of ethical claims and the force of moral arguments by having everything dissolve into the exigency of the purely local and the contingency of changing customs and perspectives? Does this not open the floodgates to a rampant relativism in which all criteria for moral action are divested of obligatory force and every perspective, every interpretation, and every moral point of view is considered as good as and no worse than any other perspective, interpretation, and moral point of view? Does this not lead simply and straightforwardly to a historical relativism in which no claims, either of an epistemic or a moral sort, transcend the historically specific?

This issue has appeared in different forms throughout the long history of occidental thought, and has been flagged variously as the "problem of relativism," the "problem of historicism," and the "problem of nihilism"—and more generally as a very big problem involving all three. But this problem that appears to elicit so much attention is formulated both in its design and its anticipated resolution as a *theoretical* problem. It is theory—ethical theory, moral theory, social theory, theory of culture—that is called upon to settle the dispute. And the dispute is framed, as philosophical disputes commonly are, in terms of a conceptual either/or—*either* the theory of relativism *or* the theory of absolutism, *either* the theory of historicism *or* the theory of universalism, *either* the theory of nihilism *or* the theory of a priori values. Much ado about theory clearly is going on here, and what is asked of the either/or is that it induce us to make a choice for one theory as opposed to another.

From time to time, those trafficking in theory construction, and interested onlookers, have become dismayed that no resolution to this long-standing problem has been forthcoming. Indeed, there are those who find it scandalous that philosophers throughout the ages have lacked the requisite resources for coming up with the criteria on the basis of which to make a rational decision in the face of this all-important theoretical either/or. Might it be, however, that what is troublesome, disconcerting, or even scandalous is not that no correct theory for resolving the problem has yet surfaced, but rather that the conceptual construction of the issue has somehow been sold as a *genuine problem* and that "correct" theories continue to be sought?

Let us suppose that what the times require is not a new conceptual scheme and an accompanying argument for enfranchising one or the other of the theoretically posited polar opposites (relativism contra absolutism, historicism contra universalism, and nihilism contra a priori values), but rather a recognition that the posited polar opposites rest on a bogus dichotomy that is created by the requirement of theory to lay out criteria of justification in advance of the specific practices to which such criteria might apply. Let us suppose that the either/or that provides the occasion for both personal and social morality is not of a theoretical sort at all. Let us suppose further that the obsession with methodology and criteriology, which has driven so much of the philosophical inquiry of modernity, has run its course.

Against the backdrop of these suppositions one would do well to recommend a shift from theory to praxis, from antecedent rule-governed criteria to context-informed criteria, to an either/or that no longer stands in wait of a theory to swoop down from on high but instead is firmly ensconced within the everyday communicative practices where life's decisions take place. In the thought experiment with such a recommendation we have much to learn from the philosophy of William James, and more specifically from his pragmatic approach to the meaning and function of *options* as they play themselves out in dealing with either/or situations. Clarifying the semantics of *option,* James distinguishes three sorts — living or dead, forced or avoidable, and momentous or trivial. An option is *genuine* for James only when it is at once living, forced, and momentous. A living option has to do with the presentment of alternative hypotheses, both of which elicit in the deliberator a propensity to assent. For an option to be forced, it has to close off the possibility of avoiding a decision. And finally, an option is momentous rather than trivial when it offers an opportunity that is unique and when the decision concerning it is irreversible, even if it later is considered to have been unwise. James provides specific examples of living, forced, and momentous options. "Be an agnostic or be a Christian" James considers to be a living option because the two hypotheses have the power to elicit a believing tendency among their hearers. For James liveness and deadness are not intrinsic properties that somehow attach to hypotheses and options, but are determined contextually, vis-à-vis the disposition of the interlocutor and his or her cultural background of beliefs and practices. As an example of a forced option James submits "Either accept this truth or go without it." It is forced because one cannot straddle the middle.

In postponing the decision, one goes without the truth for at least the time being. As an illustration of a momentous option, James suggests the option of joining Dr. Nansen for a North Pole expedition, which affords a chance of a lifetime. The wider project, in whose service James's semantic analysis of the three kinds of options stands, is to show that moral and religious issues are matters of living, forced, and momentous options and require decisions based on pragmatic considerations rather than theoretical demonstrations.[17]

Of particular interest in James's account is his telling example of an option that does not qualify as genuine because it fails to require a decision: "Either call my theory true or call it false." In this case judgments about the viability of the theory can be postponed until further evidence is forthcoming. Or one might devise a third theory and begin to look for some loyal supporters, or one might simply decline to offer any judgments about the theory. The point is that in dealing with a theoretical either/or one can place oneself outside the alternatives and withhold judgment. A theoretical option is avoidable rather than forced. And within James's scheme of things we would also need to consider theoretical options, at least as they pertain to our moral and religious life, as trivial rather than momentous. They do not solicit decisions that make a vital difference in the moral life of the self in its communalized existence. The theoretical either/or traffics in the realm of conceptual schemes rather than in the economy of public concerns. Such an either/or, which is unable to fulfill the conditions for a genuine option as characterized by James, needs to be contrasted with a pragmatic and existential either/or. An existential either/or calls for a quickened response to the voice and action

17. William James, *The Will to Believe* (New York: Dover Publications, 1956), pp. 1–31.

of the other within the rough and tumble of lived-through experience, where the voice of the other is often a cry for help by a child living in abject poverty and the action of the other a request for intervention to forestall blatant discrimination.

In analyzing the dynamics of an existential either/or, one finds that it is coupled with an existential doubt that needs to be distinguished from the methodological doubt that is called upon to adjudicate in deciding for one theoretical alternative over another. Methodological doubt is hyperbolic and abstract, bent on the justification of beliefs and cognitive claims on the basis of antecedentally stipulated criteria. The doubt that accompanies an existential either/or and its call for decision is a doubt driven by the urgency to make choices that bear directly on the future of the human self in its interdependent existence with other selves. It is a doubt impelled by a search for the meaning of personal and social existence within the arena of practical wisdom rather than for the meaning of propositions in the court of theoretical judgments. Theoretically defined methodological doubt is the doubt of a Descartes and a modern skeptic. Praxis-oriented existential doubt is the doubt of a Pascal and a Kierkegaard.

The proponents of theory and methodological doubt would have the criteria of justification, whether pertaining to truth and falsity or to right and wrong, laid out in advance. This defines the Cartesian prejudice of determining the rules of method prior to the actual investigation of events and processes — events and processes of mind as well as events and processes of matter. In contrast, the criteria that are called upon in decisions induced by the existential doubt in a praxis-rooted either/or are not antecedently defined and legislated in advance of the investigative process. They are the progeny of the discernment and deliberation that accompanies the contrastive comparisons at play in the lifeworld of human interactions. Criteria are as much constituted by the events and processes in the lifeworld as they are a judge of them, attesting to a continuing dialectic of constitution and evaluation.[18]

Viewing criteria for evaluation as contemporaneous with the occurrence of events and processes to be evaluated does not mean that criteria for judging that which is fitting in one's responses to prior discourse and action are merely arbitrary or purely relativistic, as the protagonists of absolutism would be disposed to claim. In their role of supplying resources for critical evaluation and grounds for critique, criteria are *conditioned* by historically specific contexts, but they are not *determined* by such contexts. The failure to distinguish between "context-conditioned" and "context-determined" has ushered in a profound confusion on matters of the degree and quality of transcendence required for making moral judgments and submitting critiques of culture. That a configuration of thought or action is conditioned or informed by its context is not tantamount to its being determined by its context.

Conditioned by its context, human thought is nonetheless able to transcend the particularities of its social and historical inherence, stand back, establish a distance from both traditional and occurrent practices, suspend beliefs about them, re-

18. The problematizing of antecedentally defined criteria not only applies to the culture-spheres of morality and art, where ethical and aesthetic judgments are tightly woven into the narratives told by the community and conditioned by the contingencies of social practices, but is equally problematic in projects of scientific research and discovery. Paul Feyerabend, discussing the dynamics of scientific inquiry, observes that "criteria do not merely *judge* events and processes, they are often constituted by them and they must be introduced in this manner or else research will never get started" (*Farewell to Reason* [New York: Verso Press, 1987], p. 283). This assessment provides further support for our general argument that the lines of division between science, morality, and art have been too sharply drawn by the prophets of modernity.

vise and revamp some, and completely overturn others. It is this refusal to be determined by a particular tradition, a particular conceptual system, or a particular form of behavior that enables a standpoint of critique that delivers us from a relativism and a hermeneutical anarchy in which all interpretations and perspectives are granted an equal claim to thrive because they are simply determined by their particular place in society and their particular time in history. Herein resides the mistake of all relativisms, historicisms, and nihilisms, equating the context-conditioned with the context-determined.

But the appeals to universal, unconditioned, and context-independent norms and principles by the antihistoricist absolutists simply reflect the obverse side of the same mistake. Assuming that contextuality entails determinism, closing all forms of transcendence, the absolutist appeals to a priori and context-free conditions to provide a standpoint of critique that is not delimited by the historically specific. Whereas the relativist embraces contextuality and contingency in the mistaken belief that no transcendence of the contextualized and contingent particular practices is possible, the absolutist harbors the same mistaken notion about contextuality and contingency and yearns for a foundationalist universality and necessity wherewith to ground a transcending critique that is wholly contextless.

The bogus dichotomies of the absolute versus the relative, the universal versus the particular, the necessary versus the contingent, and the ahistorical versus the historical need to be recognized for what they are—namely, conceptual constructs of a theoretical position-taking that are no longer compelling, options bereft of practical consequences for an understanding of ourselves and our world. Yet, the interests and intentions on the part of the protagonists and antagonists in the recurring intellectualized disputes have their own positive story to tell. The intent on the part of the ahistorical absolutist to safeguard the validity of thought and the efficacy of critique is laudable, as is the intent of the historical relativist not to lose sight of the bearing of social practices in the shaping of the human mind. But the affirmation of the one intent does not entail a negation of the other. Truth claims and effective critique remain in force after the allegiance to pre-given necessary conditions and rules on the part of theoretical critique is jettisoned and the context-conditioned is no longer equated with the context-determined. The space of such truth claims and effective critique is the space of a communicative praxis, transversely textured, enabling a transhistorical assessment and evaluation to guide a fitting response that is neither ahistorically absolutist nor historically relativistic.

The self in community is a self situated in this space of communicative praxis, historically embedded, existing with others, inclusive of predecessors, contemporaries, and successors. Never an island entire of itself, the self remains rooted in history but is not suffocated by the influx of historical forms and forces. The communalized self is *in* history but not *of* history. It has the resources for transcending the historically specific without arrogating to itself an unconditioned and decontextualized vision of the world.

4

The Self in Transcendence

The fourth and final chapter of this book is designed as a thought experiment on the status and dynamics of the self in transcendence. To be sure, the topic of transcendence has been on the horizon in the previous investigations of the self in discourse, the self in action, and the self in community. It has been implicit throughout, obliquely referenced at various junctures, playing the role of a sort of underlaborer. In this chapter the profile of transcendence will be placed on center stage, supplying the project of elucidating the fortunes of the self in the aftermath of postmodernist critique with a semblance of closure.

Some general comments on the semantics of transcendence will, it is hoped, aid us in wending our way through some of the conceptual thickets. Even for the casual observer, the phenomenon of transcendence appears as a labyrinth of multiple senses, differing perspectives, conflicting interpretations, and variegated experiences. Hence, there is a need, in the interests of terminological clarification and reduction of ambiguity, to sort out some of the different senses of the concept of transcendence—a concept that in the history of philosophy and religion has not had the good fortune of achieving a univocal meaning.

Surely meanings of terms and phrases have much to do with their usage. And senses of transcendence have already been operant in our discussions of the self in discourse, the self in action, and the self in community. This is but another indicator that the four profiles in our sketch of the portrait of the self after postmodernity are to be properly understood as interwoven perspectives rather than as serial and incremental developments.

Transcendence was announced in the discussion of the self in discourse, in developing the point that language transcends every particular speech act. When one speaks, one speaks from a language that has already delivered a surplus of significations. It is in this sense that one can speak of language as being transcendent. It is transcendent to the act of speaking. Although language, both as a formal system and as a historical development, becomes incarnate in the spoken word, its resources are inexhaustible in any historically specific articulations. Transcendence is also operative in the self-constituting action of the engaged subject. Action is precisely the going over and moving beyond the present state of affairs to that which is yet to be done. The self in action is a self in transcendence—moving beyond that which it has become and going over to that which it is not yet. And finally, transcendence is in play in the dialectic of self and community insofar as the self understands itself in its encounter with other selves and in its engagement with a tradition that antedates its self-constitution. Transcendence is operant not only in the face-to-face encounter with the other self as other, but also in the self's recognition that the totality of received social practices exceeds its particular hold on the world. The holistic matrix and referential interdependence of social practices and communal involvements transcend the particular discourses and actions of embodied agents.

Clearly, different senses of transcendence travel with each of these profiles. In the case of discourse, transcendence refers to a cultural content—language as both a semiotic system and a historical development. In the case of action, transcendence is indicative of an act or project of transcending; it functions more like a verb than like a noun. In the case of the self in community, transcendence is activated against the backdrop of the whole-part distinction. Yet, there are family resemblances among these different senses, involving different takes on the relevance of alterity, the impingement of that which is other — including other cultural contents, other narratives, other interpretations, other selves, other configurative complexes of social practice, and so on. Transcendence thus appears to find a close cognate in "that which is other." But these senses of otherness are still quite mundane and domesticated. They remain within the household, the economy, of distribution-and-exchange relations of discourse, action, and intersubjective associations. They make up what one might call the weaker sense of the transcendence-alterity coupling, legitimating talk of a transcendence-within-immanence. It is this sense of transcendence to which Husserl appealed when insisting that the "perceived object" is not to be confused with the "object-as-perceived" or the "object-as-meant." Consciousness for Husserl *constitutes the meaning of objects;* it does not *create the objects* in the experienced lifeworld. The perceived object transcends the object-as-perceived. The blinding light is other than the experience of the glare by an intending consciousness. Yet, this alterity of the blinding light remains operant within the immanental structure of consciousness-experiencing-the-world.

A distinction akin to Husserl's distinction between the perceived object and the object-as-meant has been offered by Gilbert Ryle, albeit from a perspective of linguistic analysis rather than that of an analytic of consciousness. In our everyday language use, Ryle observes, we are prone to speak of seeing the "house from the front" rather than seeing the "front of the house." Now, there is an implied truth of perception in this ordinary linguistic practice. Perception is a matter of apprehending worldly objects from different perspectives rather than a matter of maneuvering abstracted sense-data by, for example, having a sense datum of "front" and then appealing to some species of rules of inference to enable one to move to a "back," a "side," a "top," a "bottom." As Husserl's perceived object transcends the object-as-meant, so Ryle's full-bodied, perceived "house from the front" transcends the "front of the house" as an abstracted sensory quality. Perception itself testifies of a transcendence-within-immanence.[1]

There is, however, also a sense of transcendence that is coupled with an alterity that exceeds the bounds of the economy of intramundane forms of transcendence. This is the sense of transcendence that has been given a hearing in the metaphysical tradition whenever there has been talk about Platonic transcendent forms, a Kantian noumenal realm, or God as an infinite and supremely perfect being in the several varieties of classical theism. The defining feature of this notion of transcendence is unconditioned and nondependent existence—a feature that receives support from a rather bold application of the metaphysical categories of substance and causality. In its purest metaphysical guise the transcendent is that which exists

1. For a discussion of the contribution of the school of ordinary language philosophy to the phenomenological analyses of Husserl's concept of the lifeworld (*Lebenswelt*) see John Wild, "Is There a World of Ordinary Language?" *Philosophical Review*, vol. 67, no. 4, 1958. Husserl's and Ryle's distinctions relative to the life of perception are similar to some of the more recent literature on the topic. A case in point is Fred Dretske's distinction between nonepistemic and epistemic seeing (see his book *Seeing and Knowing* [Chicago: University of Chicago Press, 1969]). But Dretske moves too quickly from the nonepistemic to the epistemic and thus is unable to grant to nonepistemic seeing (seeing as it is operative in the concrete lifeworld) its proper integrity. The space of nonepistemic seeing functions at best as an anteroom to honest-to-goodness epistemic seeing, as nonepistemic seeing is destined to wait upon complicated epistemological conditions to take on the determinations of knowledge. But it is precisely from such theoretico-epistemological pre-conditions that the later Wittgenstein, Ryle, and Austin delivered us.

in and through itself alone, separated from the realm of immanence defined as that which exists only by virtue of the external causal agency of another. In the history of the theometaphysics of classical theism, the being of God exemplifies such a nature. God as infinite, immutable, and supremely perfect enjoys an existence that is unqualifiedly unconditioned and nondependent, absolutely constitutive of everything finite; and everything finite within the realm of immanence remains absolutely nonconstitutive of God as infinite. It may be useful to name this view of transcendence *metaphysical* transcendence.

Such a notion of transcendence, metaphysically construed, would clearly qualify as transcendence in the strong sense, distinguishing this use of the term from its usage in a weaker sense. What is at issue is no longer a transcendence-within-immanence, a transcendence within the economies of the human subject understanding itself in its discourse, action, perception, and communal involvements, but rather transcendence as an encounter with what Emmanuel Levinas has appropriately named a "radical exteriority."[2] This is transcendence understood as residing on the other side of the economies of human experience—and yet playing a role, and possibly a pivotal role, in the drama of self-constitution, in the attestation of the self as constituted in and through its relation to the radically transcendent.[3]

Additional examples of the grammar and understanding of

2. For some of the more explicit statements by Levinas on the status and function of transcendence as "absolute exteriority" see *Totality and Infinity: An Essay on Exteriority,* trans. Alphonso Lingis (Pittsburgh: Duquesne University Press, 1960), particularly the section titled "Transcendence as the Idea of Infinity," pp. 48–52.

3. See also in this context Søren Kierkegaard's description of the self as a dialectical synthesis of infinity and finitude in *The Sickness unto Death,* trans. Walter Lowrie (Princeton: Princeton University Press, 1951).

transcendence in the strong sense might further clarify this conceptually slippery notion. The history of mysticism, and particularly of the representative mystics in the tradition of Western philosophy and religion, provides illustrations of the strong sense of transcendence: the ineffable "One" of Plotinus, the "Godhead" of Meister Eckhart, and the "Holy Trinity" of Saint John of the Cross. The reports and elucidations of the mystical encounter as experienced by these representatives at times lean heavily on the metaphysical grammar of the Western philosophical tradition, which gives some credence to the view that the mystical continues to reside in the metaphysical.

Another example of transcendence in the strong sense, but one that is less reliant on metaphysical binaries, is Rudolph Otto's phenomenological elucidation of the idea of the Holy (*Das Heilige*). The elements of the "*numinous*" and the "*mysterium tremendum*," which punctuate the disclosure of the Holy, are clearly lexical indicators of a radical transcendence, for which the quintessential expression is the "wholly other" (*totaliter aliter*). Yet, we flag this strong sense of transcendence as being less informed by metaphysical categories than the previously discussed mystical sense because the relation between the Holy and the profane as articulated by Otto has more to do with an unfathomable depth within the dynamics of religious experience than with a relation of cause and effect. The experience of the Holy is a matter of encounter rather than of inference, informed by the self-disclosure of an alterity that invades the intentional structure of intramundane perception and evaluation. Although the categories that service the understanding of the intramundane world-regions are not as such annulled, the numinous quality of the Holy remains conceptually unknowable and requires for its being experienced a bracketing of the intramundane varieties of experience—perceptual, aesthetical, and even ethical. The experience of the Holy is qualified as little as possible by everyday forms of consciousness. Its status as a marker of that which is wholly other is determined by the uniqueness of religious experience rather than by the outcome of a metaphysical argument.

A third example of transcendence in the strong sense can be found in the existential philosophy of Karl Jaspers, where it is given an expression in his doctrine of the "Encompassing" (*Das Umgreifende*). This doctrine is elaborated in a dense chapter in one of Jaspers's more important works, *Reason and Existenz*. The vocabulary that Jaspers uses to develop his notion of the Encompassing remains heavily indebted to classical German Idealism, from Kant through Hegel. Yet, Jaspers is not simply a filial descendent of this tradition. His project can be understood, at least from a historical perspective, as an effort to elucidate the existential underpinnings that informed the origin and development of classical continental rationalism, and the history of Western philosophy from Socrates onward. Transcendence, described by Jaspers as a mode of the Encompassing, functions as the ultimate limit to rational comprehension.[4] It is that to which no concepts can move and beyond which none can proceed. It is a "transcendence which shows itself to no investigative experience, not even indirectly." Like the noumenal realm in the thought of Kant, transcendence for Jaspers "remains unseen and unknown."[5] As objectively unknowable

4. Jaspers's doctrine of the Encompassing, defined as periechontology, is sketched in Karl Jaspers, *Reason and Existenz,* trans. William Earle (London: Routledge and Kegan Paul, 1956), and particularly in "Second Lecture: The Encompassing," pp. 51-76.

5. *Reason and Existenz,* p. 60. For helpful discussions of Jaspers's views on transcendence see Leonard H. Erlich, *Karl Jaspers: Philosophy as Faith* (Amherst: University of Massachusetts Press, 1975), and Oswald O. Schrag, *Existence, Existenz, and Transcendence: An Introduction to the Philosophy of Karl Jaspers* (Pittsburgh: Duquesne University Press, 1971).

it can never emerge as an object or as a totality of objects. Articulated in the nonobjectivating language of ciphers, transcendence marks out the ever-receding boundary of our intramundane perspectives and conceptual schemes.

Although Jaspers does not equate transcendence with the traditional theo-metaphysical concept of God, his version of transcendence shares certain properties with this traditional concept. Because of this oblique connection with some of the designs of classical theism, Jaspers's understanding and use of transcendence must be quite sharply distinguished from that employed by Jean-Paul Sartre, even though both can be considered representatives of the existentialist tradition. Transcendence, in Sartre's existentialism, remains a form of intramundane and intratemporal self-transcendence. It defines the project of the existing self, the *pour-soi*, as a dynamic process of transcending what it has been by perpetually becoming that which it is not yet. Transcendence, for Sartre, is purely horizontal, a transcendence within the economy of self-actualization. For Jaspers transcendence is operative on two axes, a horizontal and a vertical, at once defining the structure of self-actualization and marking out an encounter with an indeterminate range of the possible beyond all world horizons.

These examples, which are something of a mixed bag, provide, it is hoped, the requisite clarification of a strong sense of transcendence as it has been given expression in the tradition from the ancients to the moderns. In this concluding chapter an effort will be made to refigure the semantics of transcendence in its strong sense, dismantling its metaphysical underbelly while reconstructing the intent of its metaphysical ruminations. And this will be done, in part at least, through a reminiscence on Kierkegaard, recalling his imaginative construal of the category of repetition as that which "is the *interest* of metaphysics, and at the same time the interest upon which metaphysics founders."[6] In an analogous manner the refigured notion of transcendence proposed in what follows retains the existential concern and interest in the asking of the metaphysical question while dismantling the sedimented constructs of theo-metaphysical speculation.

To begin the narrative of the refiguration of the semantics of transcendence with an account of the contribution of Kierkegaard is to embark on a wider story of the Kierkegaard-effect in the shaping of the contours of modernity, and particularly as this effect played itself out in the demarcation of the so-called culture-spheres of modern thought. The received definition of modernity specifies science, morality, and art as the cardinal constituents of modern culture. These cultural constituents are viewed as disjoined, split off from each other. Max Weber spoke of the separation of the three culture-spheres as a "stubborn differentiation." Habermas has accepted this received definition of modernity and the stubborn differentiation thesis as framed by Weber, and he has sought to rectify the problems consequent to this differentiation with a theory of communicative rationality that binds the validity claims within science, morality, and art without reducing any one to the other.[7]

What is missing in this received account of the problem of modernity, and Habermas's aggressive effort to solve it, is

6. Søren Kierkegaard, *Repetition: An Essay in Experimental Psychology*, trans. Walter Lowrie (New York: Oxford University Press, 1941), p. 34.

7. For a discussion of Habermas's framing of the problem of modernity, and his views on the unsuccessful efforts by Hegel to solve it, see *The Philosophical Discourse of Modernity*, trans. Frederick Lawrence (Cambridge: MIT Press, 1987), pp. 40, 74. Habermas's consummate theory of communicative rationality, with its elaborate doctrine of the different validity claims operative in the culture spheres of science, morality, and art, is detailed in his two-volume work *The Theory of Communicative Action*, trans. Thomas McCarthy (Boston: Beacon Press, 1984 and 1987).

an account of the dynamics and role of religion in the cultural complex of modernity. Indeed, the inclusion of religion as the fourth culture-sphere may well be one of the more urgent requirements for an updating of the doctrine of the culture-spheres of modernity, with the happy consequence of learning that Kierkegaard's contribution to the issue is singularly noteworthy. In locating a place for religion in his inventory of the "stages on life's way" (the aesthetical, the ethical, and the religious), Kierkegaard already had the help of Kant. What the cartographers of the modern age tend to overlook is the importance of Kant's *Religion Within the Limits of Reason Alone* for charting the map of modernity. They trace the "problem" back to Kant's splitting apart the domains of science, morality, and art, in his three *Critiques,* but they seem oblivious to the impact of Kant's "fourth critique," the work on religion, in the making of the modern mind.

The contribution of Kierkegaard, with his trenchant narratives about the dynamics of the religious consciousness, needs to be evaluated against the backdrop of the legacy of Kant, to whom he may well have been more indebted than Kierkegaard scholars have been wont to acknowledge.[8] There are striking similarities between what Kierkegaard in his *Concluding Unscientific Postscript* named "religiousness A" and what Kant called "religion within the limits of reason alone." Both of these are definitions of religion as a "religion of immanence,"

8. A notable exception in Kierkegaard-scholarship on this issue is the book by Ronald Green, *Kant and Kierkegaard: The Hidden Debt* (Albany: State University of New York Press, 1992). Although Green's distinctly bold thesis that Kierkegaard was essentially a Kantian, who concealed his debt to Kant for a variety of reasons, may be somewhat overdrawn, the chief merit of the book is that the author calls attention to some remarkable similarities in the texts and the thoughts of these two modern philosophers.

religion as a cultural configuration of beliefs and practices tending toward institutionalization. What we are dealing with here is religion as a distinct culture-sphere, admittedly interacting in various ways with science, morality, and art, but reducible neither to any one of them nor to combined aspects of all. Religion as a culture-sphere, defined by Kant and Kierkegaard, exhibits an integrity of attitudes, beliefs, and practices that leave distinctive marks on the cultural existence of humankind.

At this juncture, however, we are still dealing with religion as a *religion of immanence*. And Kierkegaard especially wants us to be very clear about that. Matters get more interesting, but also more complicated, when one is instructed by Kierkegaard to proceed from "religiousness A" to "religiousness B." The decisive element in the procession (which in the grammar of Kierkegaard is more precisely to be understood as a leap) to religiousness B is the rupture of immanence, fracturing all efforts by the self to find the God-relationship within itself. Religiousness B finds its occasion in the encounter with a radically transcendent Other, punctuated by the incursion of the eternal into the temporal, informed by the descent of transcendence into the historical life of the subject.[9] It is the acknowledgment of the incarnation of transcendence in historical becoming that provides the answer to Climacus's soul-wrenching question in the *Philosophical Fragments* and in the *Postscript:* "How can something historical become decisive for an eternal happiness?"

At first flush it would appear that Kierkegaard is here simply voicing the classical notion of the transcendent, sketched

9. "In religiousness B the edifying is a something outside the individual—the individual does not find the edification by finding the God-relationship within himself, but relates himself to something outside himself to find the edification" (Søren Kierkegaard, *Concluding Unscientific Postscript,* trans. David F. Swenson [Princeton: Princeton University Press, 1941], p. 498).

against the backdrop of a metaphysical binarism of transcendence versus immanence. But upon closer consideration, one finds that such is not the case. Like Kierkegaard's category of repetition, so his notion of religiousness B is the "interest upon which metaphysics founders." Hence one needs to cast about for a nonmetaphysical grammar in rendering an account of the dynamics of religiousness B. This nonmetaphysical grammar is the grammar of paradox, through which alone the incursion of alterity in the odyssey of religious consciousness can be articulated. The leap of faith required by the transition to religiousness B, which plays such a prominent role in the prolific literature on Kierkegaard-interpretation, undergoes a baptism by paradox, as at once its content and mode of apprehension. The grammar of faith is the grammar of paradox. As beyond the economy of the immanental culture-spheres of science, morality, art, and religion, but still efficacious within them, the transcendence that becomes incarnate in the contingencies of historical experience takes on the lineaments of what Kierkegaard has named the Absolute Paradox.[10] Instead of a grandiose metaphysical project, juggling the categories of substance and causality, form and matter, essence and existence (which for Kierkegaard defined the misguided project of Hegel), we have a narrative of how that which is wholly other can impact on our lives.

10. The meaning and use of paradox is the centerpiece in Kierkegaard's work *Philosophical Fragments or A Fragment of Philosophy*, trans. David Swenson (Princeton: Princeton University Press, 1936). See particularly chap. 3, "The Absolute Paradox: A Metaphysical Crotchet," pp. 29–43. The use of paradox is continued in the *Postscript* to supplement the dialectics of becoming subjective. "The paradox emerges when the eternal truth and existence are placed in juxtaposition with one another; each time the stamp of existence is brought to bear, the paradox becomes more clearly evident" (*Concluding Unscientific Postscript*, p. 186).

In Kierkegaard's rendition of this narrative the function of religiousness B relative to the preceding stages of existence (the aesthetical and ethical) takes on vital importance. Kierkegaard's contributions to the issues of narrative self-identity and to the understanding of ethics as a mode or manner of praxial engagement and a life of commitment were features of his portrait of the self in its "ethical stage." The ethical stage, we recall, is but one episode of a wider scenario of life lived across the three existence-spheres of the aesthetical, the ethical, and the religious (with irony as the intermediate stage between the aesthetical and the ethical and humor as the intermediate stage between the ethical and the religious).

Now we have discovered that Kierkegaard's third existence-sphere undergoes a twofold modification into religiousness A and religiousness B. Determining the relation that obtains between the three existence-spheres, and between the two forms of religiousness in the third sphere, is a project of some magnitude and has been given its due in the burgeoning Kierkegaard-scholarship.[11] My position on this problem of interpretation, which I have developed in some detail elsewhere, is that it is a mistake to view the three stages or existence-spheres as successive developments, each supplanting the other in a linear progression toward a denouement in the attainment of a religious level of existence. They are to be understood rather as co-present profiles and intercalated dimensions of selfhood, ways of existing in the world, that inform the odyssey of the self as it exists from one moment to the next. As the ethical stage does not leave the aesthetical behind but rather refigures it, so also

11. One of the more extensive and more philosophically imaginative discussions of Kierkegaard's doctrine of the three existence-spheres can be found in Stephen N. Dunning's work *Kierkegaard's Dialectic of Inwardness: A Structural Analysis of the Theory of Stages* (Princeton: Princeton University Press, 1985).

the religious stage does not annul the ethical but rather effects its redescription.[12]

Within the format of the current investigation of the being and behavior of the self after postmodernity, Kierkegaard's doctrine of the stages proves to be particularly helpful in addressing matters germane to the modernity-versus-postmodernity disputations. This involves pursuing the bearing of Kierkegaard's three existence-spheres on the celebrated culture-spheres that inform the received definition of the modern mind. We have already problematized this received definition by using Kierkegaard (with some additional help from Kant) to eke out space for a fourth culture-sphere, roughly equivalent to what Kierkegaard came to call "religiousness A." What Kant called "religion within the limits of reason alone," Kierkegaard defined as the "religion of immanence." The point to be emphasized is that in both cases we are dealing with religion as a cultural phenomenon of institutionalized beliefs and practices.

In proceeding to Kierkegaard's religiousness B, however, matters become more complicated because we are dealing no longer with religion as a culture-sphere, with a religion of immanence, but rather with a transcendent dimension of depth. How does this dimension of transcendence stand relative to the newly articulated four culture-spheres? What effect does the radical alterity of transcendence have on the economies of science, morality, art, and religion as cultural achievements? Although the grammar of *function* is always problematic because of certain metaphysical and epistemological presuppositions that travel with it, one way of pointing to the issues

12. For a more detailed discussion of the three stages as intercalating and overlapping modes of existence see Calvin O. Schrag, *Existence and Freedom: Towards an Ontology of Human Finitude* (Evanston: Northwestern University Press, 1961), pp. 175–206.

at stake is to ask "What function does the radical alterity of transcendence perform vis-à-vis the economies of the culture-spheres?" Properly addressing this question requires a threefold response, showing how transcendence (1) occasions a standpoint for a critique and evaluation of the beliefs and practices across the spectrum of the intramundane culture-spheres of science, morality, art, and religion; (2) supplies conditions for the unification of the culture-spheres, insofar as such unification indeed becomes possible; and (3) provides resources for the transfiguration of the dynamics of self and societal formation.

Let us first address the role and function of transcendence, in its guise of radical alterity, as a critical principle. Its salient contribution in this regard is that it provides a stance or posture for a protest against aspirations toward hegemony and claims for ultimacy among the culture-spheres of science, morality, art, and religion itself. Transcendence as radical alterity functions as a principle of restraint, curbing any absolutization of methodologies, conceptual frameworks, beliefs, creeds, and institutional practices within scientific, moral, artistic, and religious endeavors. It relativizes the culture-spheres and installs a vigilance over their claims and presuppositions, curtailing any temptations to achieve a God's-eye view of the panorama of human history. Transcendence provides the requisite safeguards against ideological hegemony, irrespective of whether such hegemony has staked its claims in the sphere of science, morality, art, or institutionalized religion.

This critical principle of vigilance and protest is operative throughout the whole of Kant's "Critical Philosophy," which emerges in its broadest design as a philosophy of human finitude. And it is of particular moment that in Kant's "fourth critique," his book on religion, the critical principle is used against religion itself, that is, against religion as a cultural complex of institutionalized beliefs, practices, and rituals. This is particularly discernible in Kant's attack on clericalism, which he defines as a combination of "fetish-worship" and "fetish-faith." Fetish-worship is the condition "always found wherever, instead of principles of morality, statutory commands, rules of faith, and observances constitute the basis and the essence of the church"; and fetish-faith is the adherence to credal statutes "through which the masses are ruled and robbed of their moral freedom by subservience to a church."[13]

Kant's critique of clericalism is remarkably similar to Kierkegaard's harpooning of the established church of Denmark for its manifold foibles and hollow pretensions in his biting satire *Attack on "Christendom"* (which at times is as violent in tone as Nietzsche's *Antichrist*). Kierkegaard finds in the institutionalized Christianity of his day, which he tells us is vanguarded by a "complete crew of bishops, deans, and priests," a profound confusion of the "inventory of churches, bells, organs, benches, alms-boxes, foot-warmers, tables, hearses, etc." with the original message received by the early community of believers.[14] At times Kierkegaard's searing critique takes on the tone and weight of the prophetic denouncements of the eighth-century prophets of ancient Israel, reminiscent of the rhetoric of an Amos: "I hate, I despise your feasts . . . I will not accept your burnt offerings . . . take away your songs . . . and let justice roll down like waters, and righteousness like a mighty stream."[15]

Although the critiques of religion as a culture-sphere by Kant and Kierkegaard exhibit certain similarities, there are significant differences in the manners in which the critiques are

13. Immanuel Kant, *Religion Within the Limits of Reason Alone*, trans. T. M. Greene and H. H. Hudson (LaSalle, Ill.: Open Court Publishing, 1934), pp. 167–168.

14. Søren Kierkegaard, *Attack upon "Christendom,"* trans. Walter Lowrie (Boston: Beacon Press, 1944), pp. 29–30.

15. *Amos* 5:21–24.

launched. Kant's critique of religion proceeds from a standpoint within the bounds of reason alone. It remains an *internal* critique. It is a critique within the economy of a religion of immanence, what Kierkegaard would call "religiousness A." Although not precluding a move to Kierkegaardian "religiousness B" and its standpoint of *external* critique, Kant's approach remains within the presuppositions of a *moral* religion, from which he assesses both the negative and positive features of religion as a culture-sphere. The unique contribution of Kierkegaard resides in his delineation of a second phase of religion as an existence-sphere, namely, the phase of religiousness B. It is this second phase that brings into sharp relief the status and role of transcendence as a radical alterity. And it is this radical alterity that supplies the standpoint for an external critique of the four culture-spheres. In performing this function as a critical principle, transcendence as the voice and visage of radical alterity collaborates with the two other functions of transcendence, namely, to supply a condition for the unification of the culture-spheres and to provide a catalyst for the transfiguration of the life of self and society as it unfolds in each of the spheres.

The second function of radical transcendence pertains to its role as a condition for unification. And it is this role that speaks most specifically to the modernity problematic and the postmodern challenge to the problematic. The storm center in the modernity-postmodernity dispute pretty much revolves around the issue of unity and the question about the resources of rationality for its achievement. The architects of modernity, and particularly from Kant to Hegel and within the Age of Enlightenment more generally, defined rationality as the travail of unification. Kant located the conditions for human knowledge in a transcendental unity of apperception, whose function is that of synthesizing the forms of perception, the schemata of the imagination, and the categories of the understanding.

Hegel extended the conditions and range of human knowledge, placing further demands on the principle of unification by charting a dialectical synthesis of nature and spirit under the aegis of the telic designs of the Absolute Idea. This story of the quest for unity from Kant to Hegel provides the epistemological and metaphysical backdrop for the alleged need in the mind of modernity to solve the problem of the separation of the culture-spheres.

This need for unification is defined by the proponents of postmodernity as at once fanciful and ill conceived. The celebration of diversity, plurality, heterogeneity, and incommensurablity on the part of postmodernists renders any and all claims for unity problematic. The main challenge of sketching a portrait of the self after postmodernity is that of thinking our way through and beyond the protocols that divide the moderns and the postmoderns on the meaning and role of unity. A new perspective on transcendence can help us meet this challenge.

A positive response to the postmodern rejection of the epistemological and metaphysical spin that was put on the grammar of unity by the makers of modernity is to be recommended. The unity that is borne by the alterity of a radical transcendence is neither that of a foundationalist epistemological principle nor that of a metaphysical guarantee. It is a unity that remains outside the chief categorical schemata and supporting binary semantics of epistemological and metaphysical construction — to wit, universality, necessity, and identity versus particularity, contingency, and difference. But the jettisoning of modernity's conditions for unification does not entail a hurried displacement of the notion of unity *tout court*. What is required is a reinterpretation and redescription of the conditions for unification, pruning the criteria of modernity's demands for universality, necessity, and identity.

The project of reinterpreting and redescribing the conditions for unification follows the lead of a new application of the concept or metaphor of transversality. Admittedly, the concept of transversality has been in the lexicon of academe for some time, finding employment in the mathematical, the physical, and the life sciences. In its varied usages across the disciplines— as a generalization of orthogonality in topology, as a definition of transverse mass in nuclear physics, as a description of the networking of bands of fibers in physiology, and as a characterization of the lateral movements of vertebrae in anatomy— the function of transversality can be variously expressed as that of convergence without coincidence, conjuncture without concordance, overlapping without assimilation, and union without absorption.

It was the genius of Sartre to recognize the applicability of the concept of transversality in addressing the problem of the unity of consciousness. He rejected the later Husserl's invention of the transcendental ego as the agency of unification in the temporal flow of consciousness and offered in exchange a concrete redescription of the dynamics of unification proposed by Husserl in his analyses of retention and protention in his early work *The Phenomenology of Internal Time-Consciousness*. Sartre's redescription yields a "consciousness which unifies itself, concretely, by a play of 'transversal' intentionalities which are concrete and real retentions of past consciousness."[16] Sartre's principal point is that the postulation of a universal and timeless transcendental ego remains superfluous for an account of the unity of consciousness. Consciousness achieves unification by dint of a transversal function, an extending across and revisit-

16. Jean-Paul Sartre, *The Transcendence of the Ego: An Existentialist Theory of Consciousness,* trans. Forrest Williams and Robert Kirkpatrick (New York: Noonday Press, 1957), p. 39.

ing of past moments of consciousness without solidifying into an identification with any particular moment.

It is such a notion of unification, operating transversally in an extending across given contents, converging without becoming coincident, that can be found helpful in elucidating the unifying function of transcendence. And this is particularly the case when one is addressing the possible unification of the differentiated culture-spheres of science, morality, art, and religion. Radical transcendence operates transversally, and the salient point at issue is that the grammar of transversality replaces that of universality. The dynamics of unification in a transversal play of lying across and extending over surfaces, accelerating forces, fibers, vertebrae, and moments of consciousness is not grounded in a universal telic principle but proceeds rather as an open-textured gathering of expanding possibilities. As such it is a dynamics of unification that is always an "ing," a process of unifying, rather than an "ed," a finalized result. The unity at issue is a coefficient of thought and communication moving across differentiated belief systems, interpretive viewpoints, and regions of concern.

The achievement of unity as a transversal function is of a quite different sort than the unity that has been taken as metaphysical doctrine in Western thought. In the traditions both of the ancients and the moderns unity has fraternized with identity, and in concert unity and identity have waged war against plurality and difference. The quest for unity, as at once a metaphysical and epistemological principle, was driven by a nostalgia for a primordial and unblemished *archē*, an untrammeled beginning, and an appetition for a fixed and universal *telos*. The concept of transversal unification, in contrast, illustrates a dynamic and open-textured process of unifying that allows for plurality and difference and neither seeks the metaphysical comforts of stable beginnings and universal telic principles nor displays an epistemological enchantment with zero-point epistemic foundations.

It may be helpful to further clarify this understanding and use of transversal unification, sans universal and telic determinants, by examining illustrations of the concept in the disciplines of literary studies and organizational communication. Gilles Deleuze's essay on Proust provides a fine example of the applicability of the notion of transversality to the field of literary theory and criticism. Moving out from an examination of Proust's classic novel *A la recherche du temps perdu*, Deleuze contrasts Proustian reminiscence with Platonic recollection. Plato's doctrine of recollection is geared to the recovery of a stable and invariant idea or essence. For Plato, the "Idea as the goal of reminiscence is the stable Essence, the thing in itself separating opposites, introducing the perfect mean into the whole. This is why the Idea is always 'before,' always presupposed, even when it is discovered only afterwards." For Proust, however, reminiscence is geared to the recovery of creative viewpoints rather than pre-existent eidetic entities. Proustian reminiscence, continues Deleuze, proceeds from a "state of soul, and from its associative chains, to a creative or transcendent viewpoint—and no longer, in Plato's fashion, from a state of the world to seen objectivities."[17] Proust is thus able to proffer a more robust notion of reminiscence, in which to reminisce is not simply to recall but also to create.

The principal issue in Proustian reminiscence pertains to the structure and dynamics of unification within a remembrance of things past. What we are dealing with is a unity of viewpoints

17. Gilles Deleuze, *Proust and Signs*, trans. Richard Howard (New York: George Braziller, 1972), pp. 97–98.

rather than a unity grounded in the identity of a stable and changeless essence. Hence, Deleuze appropriately asks, "What is this very special mode of unity irreducible to any 'unification,' this very special unity which appears afterwards?" It is clearly a unity that is achieved rather than a unity somehow given beforehand, not a unity grounded in an identity of immutable sameness, but rather a unity that is the progeny of a transversal play of viewpoints. Placing the accent on what he calls the "importance of a *transversal dimension* in Proust's work," Deleuze is able to conclude that the unity at issue "is always within this dimension of transversality, in which unity and totality are established for themselves, without unifying or totalizing objects or subjects."[18] Proust's search for lost time so as to activate a remembrance of things past thus proceeds via a congruence of viewpoints without concordance, a convergence of remembered moments of time that does not congeal into a coincidence of identity.

Another helpful elucidation of the dynamics of transversal unification is found in the writings of the French philosopher and psychiatrist Félix Guattari. Guattari, who had collaborated with Deleuze on a number of occasions, including a co-authorship of the two-volume *Capitalism and Schizophrenia,* is particularly interested in the workings of transversality in the life of organizations. His concern is with the dynamics of "transversality in the group," having to do with transversal forces operative in institutional settings and organizations that are structured in terms of different constellations of power and different levels of decision making. His concrete example is that of the complex organization involved in the establishment and maintenance of a psychiatric hospital, consisting of vari-

18. *Proust and Signs,* pp. 149-150.

ous groups and subgroups, divided along the lines of degrees of technical expertise, managerial authority, and levels of concern and interest. These groups and subgroups are made up of hospital administrators, trustees, doctors, nurses, assistants to the doctors and nurses, patients, and families and friends of patients. Each of these groups displays a different social role, a different set of skills and knowledge, and a different intensity of investment of interest and concern. For optimal functioning of such a complex organization, a harmonious integration in terms of some species of unification of the different groups is required.

But this harmony and unity cannot be achieved via a vertically ordered and hegemonic decision-making arrangement that simply subordinates the lower to the higher. Nor can, of course, decision making be left to the autonomy of horizontally serialized groups, which often disagree on matters of both style and policy. What is required is a transversal ordering and communication that is achieved through a diagonal movement across the groups, acknowledging the otherness and integrity of each, while making the requisite accommodations and adjustments along the way. Such is the dynamics of transversality, striving for convergence without coincidence, skirting the Scylla of a hegemonic unification while steering clear of the Charybdis of a chaotic pluralism. Guattari sums up the guiding principle of transversality rather nicely in a consolidating statement. "Transversality is a dimension that tries to overcome both the impasse of pure verticality and that of mere horizontality; it tends to be achieved when there is a maximum of communication among the different levels and, above all, in different meanings."[19]

19. Félix Guattari, *Molecular Revolution: Psychiatry and Politics*, trans. Rosemary Sheed (New York: Penguin Books, 1984), p. 18.

What we can learn from the contributions of Sartre, Deleuze, and Guattari on the workings of transversality is that the unity that functions as a coefficient of transversality is very much an open-textured *process of unification,* moving beyond the constraints of the metaphysical oppositions of universality versus particularity and identity versus difference. Transversal unity is an achievement of communication as it visits a multiplicity of viewpoints, perspectives, belief systems, and regions of concern. It is thus that the relevance of this open-textured quality of unity for addressing the modernity problematic as it relates to the differentiated culture-spheres would appear to be quite direct. Having abandoned the search for a grounding principle of universal dimensions, which invites an overdetermination of one of the culture-spheres over the other three, we land upon the efficacy of a transcendent horizon of possibilities that ingresses into the economics of the four culture-spheres without being assimilated or absorbed into any one of them. Hence, the integrity of the historically specific discourse and action in each of the spheres is safeguarded by a radical transcendence, a horizon of otherness, an alterity of possibilities, that provides a sheet anchor against any cultural hegemony, be it that of scientism, moralism, aestheticism, or ecclesiasticism.

This understanding and application of the transversal play of transcendence has the advantage of providing an alternative to Habermas's purported resolution of what he has defined as the unacceptable differentiation of the culture-spheres in the legacy of modernity—a resolution that continues to traffic in the grammar of universalizable validity claims and context-independent conditions of ideality. Proposing a "theory of rationality with which to ascertain its own universality" whereby to ground validity claims in each of the culture-spheres that "transcend all limitations of space and time, all the provincial limitations of the given context," Habermas reverts to purchases on concepts of transcendence, rationality, unity, and universality that have outworn their usefulness in the wake of the postmodern challenge.[20] Unification no longer needs to be sought in a theory of rationality that is beholden to conditions of ideality, transcendental sources, and ideal speech situations, which are somehow context free and universally binding. Through a reanalysis of the universal into the transversal we are able to describe unification as the effecting of convergences and conjunctures across the economies of the culture-spheres without landing on any particular methodological procedure, belief system, or set of practices as universally obliging. This allows us to acknowledge the contingency and contextuality of our historically specific scientific, moral, aesthetic, and religious claims, while nurturing an appetition to see how things might hang together, however loosely. In effect, to tap the resources of transversal rationality and transversal communication is to split the difference between the demands for the solidity of an impermeable unity by the moderns and the demands for the vacuity of a porous plurality by the postmoderns.

The third function of transcendence in its guise of a radical alterity is that of providing a space and a dynamics for a transfiguration and transvaluation of the life of self and society within the intramundane culture-spheres. This third function, as Kierkegaard had already clearly discerned, involves a shift of grammar in the articulation of its significance. This shift performs a double duty. It focuses attention away from the categorial constraints of a theo-metaphysics that is destined to construe transcendence as a quasi-scientific cosmological principle, and it points to the efficacy of a transforming dynamics that

20. Jürgen Habermas, *The Theory of Communicative Action,* vol. 2, trans. Thomas McCarthy (Boston: Beacon Press, 1987), pp. 400, 399.

breaks into the economy of the four culture-spheres and transfigures their intramundane intentionalities.

It is precisely this transfigurative moment in the life of self and society that is highlighted in Kierkegaard's narrative of religiousness B with its shift of grammar from that of dialectics to that of paradox. The grammar of paradox supersedes, but does not annul, the grammar of a dialectics that remains within the limits of reason alone and which is in force in the understanding of the discourse and action within the economies of the culture-spheres. The grammar of paradox, occasioned by the particularity of the incarnation of the divine in the human, the incursion of eternity into temporal and historical becoming, points beyond the economies of the culture-spheres, which remain beholden to the metaphors of production and consumption, distribution and exchange. The semantics of self-understanding thus itself undergoes a refiguration in the struggle of the self to understand itself in its moments of transcendence.

One of the main functions of the grammar of paradox is to disassemble the metaphysical construal of the transcendent-immanent relation. The content of religiousness B, articulated through the language of faith as paradox, is not a metaphysical entity, as proposed by the proponents of classical theism. One finds no alleged proofs for the existence of a supernatural being in the writings of Kierkegaard; and this is not simply because Kierkegaard has some far-reaching reservations about the cogency of such proofs, but it is rather because the very project of a metaphysics of theism becomes problematized, deconstructed if you will, through the dynamics of "existential faith." Here much has to do with the inapplicability of "existence" to the principal referent of religious faith. "Existence" remains for Kierkegaard a category of finitude, which is stretched beyond its elastic limits when it is used in reference to the divine. "God does not think, he creates: God does not exist, he is eternal,"

Kierkegaard writes in the *Concluding Unscientific Postscript*.[21] The content of transcendence has nothing to do with the distinction between the finite and the infinite, the temporal and the eternal, the human and the divine as a metaphysical divide. The traditional metaphysical binarisms are set aside.

In his stance on the deconstruction of the metaphysics of theism, Kierkegaard is precursor to some contemporary thinkers, specifically Paul Tillich and Emmanuel Levinas. Tillich's project of "transcending theism" through an elucidation of his chief theological metaphor, the "God beyond God," presents an alternative to the dull and dreary metaphysico-epistemological exercises of attempting to prove or disprove the existence of a supernatural being. The God beyond God is the content of faith that appears in the wake of the Nietzschean diagnosis of the demise of God as a metaphysical concept. Thus, in tracking the reconstitution of the self after the postmodern pronouncement of the "death of man," we are able to see that such a reconstitution proceeds hand in glove with a relocation of the divine in the aftermath of Zarathustra's message proclaiming the "death of God."

Like Kierkegaard, Tillich considers talk of the existence of God to be bad theological grammar. Rocks exist; plants exist; animals exist; human beings exist; but the God beyond God, transcending theism, does not exist. Nor can the content of this robust transcendence be properly referenced as a "being"—not even as a being in the sense of the highest being, the *ens realissimum* of classical theism—for such would reduce the content of our "ultimate concern" to entities within the categorial schemes of our "preliminary concerns." Transcendence, for Tillich, functions as the "dimension of depth" in an ultimate concern that at once judges and regenerates the

21. *Concluding Unscientific Postscript*, p. 296.

economies of science, technology, politics, morality, art, and institutional religion—all of which are matters of preliminary concern. The content of this faith as ultimate concern, namely, the God beyond God, is quite beyond the metaphysical categories of classical theism.[22] A desirable spin-off from such a refiguration of transcendence is the displacement of the recurring theism-versus-atheism conundrum. Although affording intermittent entertainment, the frequently staged debates on whether a supernatural being indeed exists generally induce a soporific conceptual wearisomeness. Not only is the issue undecidable, the disputations continue to make purchases on a set of bogus alternatives.

A similar posture of interpretive reflection characterizes the thought of Emmanuel Levinas. Moving out from the primacy of the ethical understood as an encounter with and response to the Other as absolute exteriority, defining the ethical relation as one of asymmetry rather than reciprocity, Levinas is in position to mark out a locus of transcendence that is outside of the categories of being. In this move he is able to reclaim the pivotal perspective of the high prophetic religion of the Kingdom of Israel in the eighth century B.C. The primary question for these later Hebrew prophets was not "What are the structures of being?" but rather "What does the Lord require of you?" The ethical took precedence over the ontological, and the ethical at issue here finds its source and grounding in a radical alterity. Yet Levinas, speaking in concert with voices from his Jewish tradition, remains in a continuing conversation with the Greeks—

22. See especially Tillich's book *The Courage to Be* (New Haven: Yale University Press, 1952), particularly chap. 6, "Courage and Transcendence," pp. 155–190. See also his essay "The Lost Dimension in Religion," in *Decisions in Philosophy of Religion*, ed. W. B. Williamson (Columbus, Ohio: Charles E. Merrill Publishing, 1976).

hence the apt characterization of Levinas as a Jew-Greek or a Greek-Jew. Eighth-century Palestine and fifth-century Greece are brought into a curious juxtaposition. Zeroing in on an insight in Book VI of Plato's *Republic*, Levinas finds support for his claim regarding the transcendent source of the ethical. When Socrates informs Glaucon that the Good exceeds essence in power and dignity, we are to learn from this that before being there was the Good. Both God and the Good, as already suggested by Plato, are "otherwise than being." [23]

The contributions of Tillich and Levinas to the issue at hand —contributions that carry a significant indebtedness to Kierkegaard—demonstrate that the classical metaphysics of theism comes up lame in locating the source and dynamics of transcendence. Neither a metaphysical designator of a being in some supernatural realm nor an epistemological protocol positing conditions for knowledge (that is, the transcendent as transcendental), transcendence is more like an existential-pragmatic alterity—an alterity that registers its efficacy by making a difference in the experience of ourselves and the world. It is at once that which is other or supervenient to the configurations of experience and forms of life within the immanent culture-

23. "God is not simply the 'first other,' the 'other par excellence,' as the 'absolutely other,' but other than the other [*autre qu'autrui*], other otherwise, other with an alterity prior to the alterity of the other, prior to the ethical bond with another and different from every neighbor, transcendent to the point of absence, to the point of a possible confusion with the stirring of the *there is*" (Emmanuel Levinas, "God in Philosophy," in *Collected Philosophical Papers*, trans. Alphonso Lingis [Dordrecht: Martinus Nijhoff, 1987], pp. 165–166). See also Emmanuel Levinas, *Otherwise Than Being or Beyond Essence*, trans. Alphonso Lingis (The Hague: Martinus Nijhoff, 1981). An excellent analysis and commentary on selected aspects of the thought of Levinas has been provided by Adriaan Peperzak in *To the Other: An Introduction to the Philosophy of Emmanuel Levinas* (West Lafayette, Ind.: Purdue University Press, 1993).

spheres and that which exhibits a power to transfigure these configurations, forms, and culture-spheres. Transcendence, in the piquant vocabulary of Kierkegaard, is that which enables one to solve the "great riddle of living in eternity and yet hearing the hall clock strike."[24] It is in this riddle that the requirement for a grammar of aporia and paradox resides.

A concrete exemplification of the incarnation of transcendence, in this robust sense of alterity, in the life of self and social formation, is the paradox of giving a gift. Since the publication of Marcel Mauss's widely influential work *Essai sur le don*, a great deal of interest has been generated on the topic of the gift and the conditions for its being given. A case in point is Jacques Derrida's thought-provoking *Given Time: I. Counterfeit Money*, in which Derrida elucidates the paradox of gift-giving against the backdrop of Mauss's contribution and then continues the inquiry by framing the issue as an aporia within the relation of the gift to time. Not only does giving take place in time, but time itself, according to Derrida and Heidegger before him, takes on the lineaments of a gift.[25]

Our interest in the gift centers on its role in what we have marked out as the profile of the self in transcendence. A gift, to be genuinely a gift, is given without any expectation of return. There can be no expectation of a "countergift," for such would place the giving within the context of a contractual rather than a gift-giving relation. Certainly, if there is to be any countergift, a species of "gift exchange" if you will, the same gift that was given cannot be returned without annulling the very conditions of gift-giving, and in the end amounting to a refusal of

24. Søren Kierkegaard, *Either/Or*, vol. 2, trans. Walter Lowrie (Princeton: Princeton University Press, 1949), p. 116.

25. See Jacques Derrida, *Given Time: 1. Counterfeit Money*, trans. Peggy Kamuf (Chicago: University of Chicago Press, 1992).

the gift. This is the point made by Pierre Bourdieu in his critique of Claude Lévi-Strauss's structuralist explanation of gift exchange.[26] But even the exchange of another item, either similar or quite different, undermines the structure and dynamics of giving a gift, which needs to be freed from any expectations of return, either a return of the same or a return of that which is different. Mutatis mutandis, from the side of gift-reception, the receiver of a gift in accepting the gift needs to be freed from any obligations to reciprocate, for such would transform the gift into an incursion of a debt that requires repayment.

The point that carries the pivotal weight in the phenomenon of gift-giving and gift-receiving is that the gift as gift remains outside, external to, the economy of production and consumption, distribution and exchange. Indeed, the gift remains radically transcendent to the determinations of reciprocity within the economy of goods and services; and insofar as it does impinge upon and interact with this economy, the gift displays a surplus of significations that overflow the particulars within the cycle of putative gift exchange. This applies not only in the giving of goods but also in the rendering of services, in the helping of a friend in need, in the offering of words of counsel and encouragement, in the paying of a visit through the giving of one's presence. In all this the paradoxical nature of gift-giving and gift-receiving becomes manifest. The gift is outside the economy, both economy in the narrower sense of monetary management and in the broader sense of motivating forces and requirements of reciprocity and exchange in the culture-spheres of scientific, artistic, ethico-moral, and religious-institutional endeavors. Yet, the giving and receiving of gifts take place within these economies. The gift is both transcendent to and

26. Pierre Bourdieu, *Outline of a Theory of Practice* (Cambridge: Cambridge University Press, 1977), p. 5.

immanent within the developing culture-spheres in which the human self aspires toward a self-understanding.

A careful reading of Kierkegaard's existence-sphere of religiousness B will set forth the source and dynamics in the paradox of gift-giving and gift-receiving, which is at once transcendent and immanent, operative within the economies of human endeavor but living off resources that are supervenient or advential, resources that issue from a power tempered by a *caritas,* a charity, that expects no reimbursement. Kierkegaard called this power the "works of love," a phrase with which he saw fit to title one of his most important books. The love at issue here, which works itself out in the economy of loving one's neighbor as oneself, is a love that finds its ultimate motivation and efficacy in a love that is freely given; a love that loves for the sake of loving; a nonpossessive love; a love that loves in spite of being unrequited; a love that expects nothing in return. The working of such a love is that which most poignantly tells the story of the profile of the self in transcendence.[27]

In seeking to comprehend the force and effects of the transcending power of love as elucidated by Kierkegaard, it is essential not to lose sight of its genuinely paradoxical texture. The love at issue, we are given to understand, is indeed a neighborly love, a love of compassionate friendship, "charity" in the originative sense of *caritas.* As such it recalls at once the Aristotelian teaching on friendship (*philia*) and the Augustinian doctrine of caritas as informed by *agapē,* a love that issues from a power to love in spite of rejection, a love that loves for the sake of loving. That Kierkegaard had a profound respect for Aristotle's interpretation of friendship as a pivotal feature of the ethical stage is well documented. Kierkegaard finds in the idea of friendship

27. Søren Kierkegaard, *Works of Love,* trans. David Swenson and Lillian Swenson (Princeton: Princeton University Press, 1946).

as developed by Aristotle a leavening of the demands of justice and a clear recognition of the relevance of the social, neither of which had a place in modern deontological ethical theories, which attempt to ground justice on duty and its categorical imperatives.[28]

But coupled with this recollection of Aristotle's notion of friendship in Kierkegaard's hermeneutic on the works of love there is a quite explicit reclamation of the New Testament and Augustinian teachings on agapē and caritas, in which love is construed as freely given and nonpossessive in nature. And it is the Augustinian view that brings into relief the limitations of Aristotle. Aristotle's idea of friendship remains rooted in the requirements for reciprocity. Philia is possible only between equals, says Aristotle. Friends mirror each other in their beliefs and practices in the exercise of mutuality and reciprocity. But the workings of love as freely given with no expectation of return transcend the occurrent ruptures of the reciprocity upon which friendship itself is built. The brotherly love of friendship, reliant on its own resources, remains bound to the category of the ethical. But the ethical stage, as Kierkegaard repeatedly reminds us, remains truncated and partial without the paradoxical intervention of the gift of love in the leap to religiousness B.

The works of love, as elucidated by Kierkegaard, do indeed provide a glimpse of life lived beyond the ethical existence-sphere and beyond good and evil as moral categories within the network of societal distribution and exchange relations. The

28. "How did Aristotle interpret friendship? Did he not make this the starting-point for his whole ethical view of life? For with friendship, he says, the concepts of justice are so broadened that they coalesce with it. He bases the concept of justice upon the idea of friendship. His category is thus in a certain sense more perfect than the modern view which bases justice upon duty, the abstract categorical—he bases it upon the social sense" (*Either/Or*, vol. II, p. 269).

dynamics of love, as unconditional and in excess of the bounds of reciprocity, involves not only a *teleological* suspension of the ethical (as defined in Kierkegaard's reading of the Abraham and Isaac saga in *Fear and Trembling*); it also propels a *deontological* suspension of the ethical (as illustrated in the requirement to move beyond Judge William's ethic of duty in volume 2 of *Either/Or*). Commentators and critics have been taken by Kierkegaard's notion of the teleological suspension of the ethical, but they have tended to gloss over his critique of deontological ethics. The efficacy of a nonpossessive love supersedes the conditions and constraints of both teleological and deontological ethics. Kierkegaard's *Fear and Trembling* and his *Either/Or* need to be read against the backdrop of his *Works of Love*.

Love as elucidated by Kierkegaard is never simply the motivating force in deliberation on how to achieve certain ends, nor is it reducible to an obligation to perform a duty at the beckoning of a categorical imperative. It cannot be defined in terms of prescriptions for self-realization attuned to pre-determined ends of nature, nor is it based on the dictates of a moral law. It transcends both an ethic of virtue and a morality of unconditional imperatives. Hence, the ethical and moral theories of both Aristotle and Kant, and the teleological and deontological traditions of ethical theory construction more generally, come up short in guiding one through the stages on life's way.

As one lives the life of transcendence in Kierkegaard's stage of religiousness B, the grammar of norm and law is replaced by the grammar of grace and gift. It is the giving and receiving of gifts, and pre-eminently the gift of love, that relativizes and subordinates teleological and deontological requirements alike. This is why love is neither a telic norm nor able to be commanded. Although made explicit in *Works of Love*, this teaching was already present in Kierkegaard's existential hermeneutic of the saga of Abraham and Isaac in *Fear and Trembling*.

Isaac was a gift to Abraham and Sara, miraculously given after Sara's childbearing years, and then he was given again following Abraham's steadfastness in the ordeal of testing on Mount Moriah, through which a potential murder was transformed into a transcendent act of faith. At the end of the saga, Abraham still had Isaac, or more precisely had Isaac returned to him after having lost him in the command that he be sacrificed. But consequent to his leap of faith he had Isaac in a new way, in a new mode of existence, no longer under the aegis of the requirement of the ethical but rather through an understanding of the giving of a gift that suspends and then transfigures the economy of the ethical itself.

Within the perspective of Kierkegaard's doctrine of the existence-spheres, we are thus able to see how the religious sphere moves "beyond" the ethical sphere. Yet, we are reminded that the advance from the aesthetical to the ethical and from the ethical to the religious is not a serial progression in which the former is somehow left behind. The aesthetical, the ethical, and the religious are constitutive and complementary cross-sections of the self in its historical becoming. So the ethical remains within the religious, but by dint of the qualification of the religious as the transcendence of religiousness B, the relation of the ethical to the religious can be articulated only in the grammar of paradox. In the economy of religiousness A, the economy of moral religion as a religion of immanence, love requires institutionalization as a commandment: "Thou shalt love thy neighbor." But love as a gift that is freely given cannot be commanded, and as such involves not only a paradoxical suspending of the ethical, but also a transgressing of the edicts and commands of institutionalized religion.

One is thus able to speak of the freely given gift of love as *transcending religion itself*—that is, transcending religion as a sphere of immanence, a culture-sphere alongside the culture-spheres of science, morality, and art. Hence, the issue is no longer simply that of finding in the resources of transcendence an answer to the traditional problem of the relation of morality to religion; the sphere of religion itself suffers a relativization of its historically specific and institutionalized beliefs and practices as it stands before the alterity of the gift of transcendence. The gift is orthogonal to each of the historical institutions of religion and transversally extends across them. Although the belief systems, symbols, and religio-moral prescriptions of the particular historical religions—such as Judaism, Christianity, and Islam in the West and Hinduism, Buddhism, and Taoism in the East—are not as such invalidated, they are nonetheless transcended and given notice of the snares of idolatry. The beliefs and practices of a particular religion become idolatric when they issue from claims for absoluteness and ultimacy. The religious qualification of the gift-giving feature of transcendent love, the posture of "being religious," should never be identified with the principles and edicts of "a religion." The condition of being religious as the depth dimension of unconditional love is older than religion itself. Yet, the dynamics of love can be efficacious in the life of a particularized, historical religion. So religion as a culture-sphere is not annulled in the encounter with transcendence. It is reclaimed and refigured in its relativity. In an analogous manner, the culture-sphere of ethics is not displaced or somehow left behind, but undergoes a transvaluation. The "fittingness" that provides the principal ingredient of the ethical sphere, defining the ethical in terms of an ethic of the fitting response, is lifted out of the requirements of reciprocity, is tempered by a love that is unconditional, and then descends back into the economy of intramundane concerns and preoccupations.

Discourse about the ways of love requires experimentation with different vocabularies in efforts to articulate love's workings on the borders of transcendence and immanence. To that end Kierkegaard was compelled to speak of an Absolute Paradox that announced the incarnation of unconditional love within the public affairs of everyday life. Levinas had recourse to the grammar of "ambiguity" in his epistle "The Ambiguity of Love," in which we are taught that "love, which as transcendence goes unto the Other, throws us back this side of immanence itself," and that the dynamics of its adventure "brings into relief the ambiguity of an event situated at the limit of immanence and transcendence."[29] It is precisely in dealing with matters of transcendence relative to the ingression of unconditional love into the economies of the conditioned culture-spheres that the labors in a cross-reading of Kierkegaard and Levinas offer their own intrinsic rewards.

Such a cross-reading would not only uncover some remarkable similarities between representatives of different religions, but it would also nurture a transversal communication that struggles to maintain itself across often-diverging viewpoints. That there are lines of convergence between the Christian religious consciousness of a Kierkegaard and the Jewish religious consciousness of a Levinas is apparent. When Levinas speaks of love as a transcendence that reaches to the Other and then reverberates back to the side of immanence, his words could be attributed to Kierkegaard as well. That one can find among representatives of the Western religions of Christianity and Judaism a common ground in the notion of transcending love may not come as much of a surprise. But teachings of transcendence and love do not appear to be restricted by geographical boundaries separating East and West. The literatures of the religions of the East have their own stories to tell about the ways of transcendence as exemplified in the works of love. Western religions

29. *Totality and Infinity*, p. 254.

do not have a monopoly on transcendence as gift-giving. In the writings of Keiji Nishitani, for example, the notion of love as Compassion is elucidated as a central teaching of Buddhism. And it is surely of some consequence that Nishitani's elucidation of compassion proceeds in tandem with commentaries on the homilies of Saint Francis of Assisi and Kierkegaard's *Works of Love*.[30]

Yet, it is important to proceed with caution in search for a common ground on matters of transcendence as one moves across the different expressions of Western and Eastern religion. The hope of finding a common denominator for the beliefs and practices among the different world religions, often cultivated by studies in comparative religion, is a hope destined for disappointment. Cultural differences pertaining to belief systems and ethnic traditions always travel with the institutionalization of religion. Therefore a cross-reading of accounts by representatives of the world religions will yield not only striking similarities but also significant differences, providing an invitation to understand the self in transcendence against the background of divergent perspectives, giving due regard to the in-

30. I am indebted to my colleague Donald W. Mitchell, a published scholar in the area of Eastern philosophy and religion, for calling my attention to the prominent references to transcendence and love in the Buddhist literature and, in particular, for directing me to the writings of Nishitani. See Keiji Nishitani, *Religion and Nothingness,* trans. Jan Van Bragt (Berkeley: University of California Press, 1982), pp. 272-285. In this context see also the two volumes by Robert E. Carter: *The Nothingness beyond God: An Introduction to the Philosophy of Nishida Kitar* (New York: Paragon House, 1989), and *Becoming Bamboo: Western and Eastern Explorations of the Meaning of Life* (Montreal and Kingston: McGill-Queen's University Press, 1992). For an approach to issues of transcultural understanding from the perspective of another Eastern tradition see Hwa Yol Jung, "The *Tao* of Transversality as a Global Approach to Truth: A Metacommentary on Calvin O. Schrag," *Man and World: An International Philosophical Review,* vol. 28, no. 1, 1994, pp. 11-31.

tegrity of particularity and the play of diversity. This is what I have named *transversal communication,* striving for convergence without coincidence, conjuncture without concordance, seeking to understand within the context of differences. Such transversal communication, energized by a transcendence that is older than religion itself, relativizes the belief systems of the particular historical religions and restrains overtures to ecclesiastical colonization. In such a transversal self-understanding and communication, the particular historical religions, from the East to the West, as exemplifications of the economy of religion as a culture-sphere, are called upon to use the resources of transcendence against themselves.

Transcendence in its threefold function as a principle of protest against cultural hegemony, as a condition for a transversal unification that effects a convergence without coincidence, and as a power of giving without expectation of return, stands outside the economies of science, morality, art, and religion as culture-spheres. This defines transcendence as a robust alterity. Responding to the beckoning of this otherness of transcendence, the wayfaring self struggles for a self-understanding and a self-constitution within the constraints of an irremovable finitude.

The portrait of the self that has been sketched in the course of our discussions has been designed to bring the legacy of modernity into confrontation with the sensibilities and deconstructive strategies of postmodernity. It has followed the delineations of a synchronics of self-understanding contextualized against the backdrop of a diachronics of cultural formation. The result of these delineations at the crossroads of the modern and the postmodern is a revised narrative on self-understanding and a redesigned portrait of self-formation that sets forth a who of discourse, engaged in action, communally situated, and tempered by transcendence.

Index

121, 144; existential, 135; as
ultimate concern, 137
Fanon, Frantz, 81, 85
Feuerbach, Ludwig, 6, 61
Feyerabend, Paul, 107n
finitude, 60, 62, 114n, 124, 135
forces: active and reactive, 56, 59,
100; play of, 60; exterior and
supervenient, 84–85; transversal,
131
form and matter, 3, 46, 52, 53, 121
forms of life, 29n
Foucault, Michel, 2, 38, 39n, 45, 56,
67–69, 79
freedom, 68
Freud, Sigmund, 94
friendship, 141–42
Fritzman, John, 99–100

Gadamer, Hans-Georg, 16, 18, 99
gift, 139–41, 143–45; as paradoxical,
140; and works of love, 141–43;
and faith, 144
God: concept of, 2; death of, 2,
136; and conscience, 98n; and
classical theism, 113–14; and
existential faith, 135–36; and the
"God beyond God," 136, 137
Gordon, Lewis R., 80–81
Gorgias, 30
Green, Ronald, 119n
Guattari, Félix, 131–33

Habermas, Jürgen, 5–7, 18, 80, 89,
90–91, 118, 133–34
Hegel, G. W. F., 6–7, 65, 81, 100,
116, 118n, 121, 126–27
Hegelianism, 7
hegemony, 124, 132, 148

Heidegger, Martin, xi, xii, 29, 63n,
88n, 94–95, 139
Heidelberg School, 69
hermeneutical self-implicature, 17,
60
hermeneutics, 68; of the subject,
68
heteronomy, 59
Hinduism, 145
historicism, 102–03, 108
historicity, 98
holism, 24, 71, 111
Holy, the, 115
homo narrans, 26, 39
Hume, David, 53, 83
humor, 122
Husserl, Edmund, 83–84, 112–13,
128
Hyde, Michael, 95n

Idealism, German, 116
ideology, 95, 124
I-experience, 78–80
immanence, 112–14, 120–21, 135,
138, 141, 146; religion of, 119,
123, 126, 144
incommensurability, 8, 127
individuation, 52–53
intentional fallacy, 3
intentionality, 20, 76, 82; bodily,
54; act, 57; functioning, 57; of
embodiment, 62
interpretation, 93
intersubjectivity, 88, 101
irony, 122
Islam, 145

James, William, 49, 71, 104–05
Jaspers, Karl, 87n, 116–17
Johnson, Mark, 23, 24, 25

ordinary language philosophy, 3, 18, 39

Otto, Rudolph, 115

Panopticon, 45

pantextualism, x, 43, 75

paradox, 121, 135, 139, 141; absolute, 121, 146; and gift-giving, 140-41

paralogy, 18n

partisans of agonistics, 18n, 30

partisans of dialogue, 18n, 30

Pascal, Blaise, 106

Peirce, Charles Sanders, 93

Peperzak, Adriaan, 138n

perception, 43-44, 55, 86, 112, 113, 126

periechontology, 116n

phenomenology, 48, 49, 51, 57, 83-84; of embodiment, 51; of the will, 60; of despair, 65

philia, 141

phonocentrism, x

phronesis, 99

Plato, 44, 45, 130, 138

Plotinus, 115

polis, 81, 86; Greek concept of, 75, 76-77, 87

politics of desire, 56

politics of marginality, 41, 72

Polkinghorne, Donald E., 23-24, 25, 37n

power: ontology of, 56; of love, 141; bio-power, 56, 62; and empowerment, 61, 62

pragmatic, 104, 105, 138

praxial critique, 99

praxial engagement, 122

praxis, 72, 76, 101, 104; commu-

nicative, 43, 44n, 61, 70-71, 73, 75, 77, 91, 109; -oriented understanding, 54, 57, 97; -oriented reason, 57

Protagoras, 30

Proust, Marcel, 130-31

psychotherapy, 24

racism, 81, 85

Ramsey, Ramsey Eric, 74n

rationalism, 116

rationality, 56-57, 133-34; communicative, 7, 90, 118; subject-centered, 7; and desire, 56-57; and power, 56-57; criteriological, 97; and unification, 126-27; transversal, 134

recollection, 130

reductionism, 26, 54, 58

reflection: and conscience, 96-97; as discernment, 97-98

relativism, 102-03, 108

religion: as culture-sphere, 6, 70, 118-23, 125-26; of immanence, 120, 123, 126, 144; as religiousness A and B, 122-23, 126, 135-36; prophetic, 137

reminiscence, 130-31

repetition, 117, 121

res cogitans, 13

res extensa, 58

responsibility, 14, 28, 64, 91-92, 98, 100, 101

responsivity, 91, 98

rhetoric, 29-30, 73-75, 76, 95n; of action, 73, 74; of discourse, 73; administrative, 75

rhetorical agonistics, 18, 30

rhizomatic, 56